FOREWORD BY TERRI

HOW TO **THRIVE** NO MATTER WHAT LIFE THROWS AT YOU

Believe
ANYWAY

ADRIENNE COOLEY

Cover design by JP Staggs

Interior design by JP Staggs

Interior composition by Adrienne Cooley

ISBN 13: 978-1-937250-67-6

For Worldwide Distribution, Printed in the U.S.A.

1 2 3 4 5 6 7 8 / 24 23 22 21

Foreword:

When I first met Adrienne Cooley in 2016, I realized a couple things. First, I found some-one who likes to smile as much as I do! But even more than that, I discovered someone who has a special gift to lift others. Because of her own journey, Adrienne has an extraor-dinary way of connecting with people at the point of their frustration or pain and walking with them step-by-step into restoration and wholeness.

And that same special gift is contained—for you—in the pages of this book, Believe ANYWAY. As you read, you're going to begin to believe God will move in your life in a greater way than ever before. In addition to her thoughtful teaching, Adrienne has includ-ed encouraging testimonies, chapter challenges to help you set goals, her H.O.P.E. meth-od to review and apply weekly Bible verses, and so much more.

As the "Cheerleader of Dreams", I've had the privilege of teaching people around the world how to make their dreams bigger than their memories and fulfill God's assignment on their lives. The sad reality is that far too many people are settling for a life below what Jesus paid to give them. They need the tools to break free and thrive; that's why I fully recommend Believe ANYWAY.

I'm a firm believer that if you can dream it, God can do it! It's time to throw off the self-im-posed restrictions and go after the God-given dreams and goals in your heart. Let this book stir your faith to believe God for big things regardless of past circumstances or setbacks. Your days ahead will be the best days of your life as you dare to step out and believe anyway!

Terri Savelle Foy | **www.terri.com**
Author of *5 Things Successful People Do Before 8 AM, Pep Talk,* and *Imagine Big*

When Adrienne Cooley began writing Believe ANYWAY, no one knew the tumultuous days we would face individually and as a nation. You will refer to this easy-to-read book filled with scripture, encouraging testimonies and easy-to-follow activity pages again and again. Your impossible situations will become possible, despair will turn into joy when you choose to Believe ANYWAY! — **Germaine Copeland** | Author of the *Prayers That Avail Much Book Series*

I fully recommend Believe ANYWAY. Adrienne has an extraordinary way of connecting with people at the point of their frustration or pain and walking with them step-by-step into restoration and wholeness. And that same special gift is contained - for you - in the pages of this book. — **Terri Savelle Foy** | Author of *5 Things Successful People do before 8 AM, Pep Talk,* and *Imagine Big* | **www.terri.com**

Adrienne asks us to believe like an innocent child, even when nothing makes sense. When the enemy says, "NO WAY that will ever happen!" Go ahead and Believe ANYWAY and watch God blow your mind! Her books are fun and colorful but also deep and full of wisdom! — **Nicole Crank** | Speaker, Author, Host of The Nicole Crank Show, & Co-Pastor of **FaithChurch.com**

I have become a lifetime fan of Adrienne's books. When I first received her books, Happy ANYWAY and Love ANYWAY, I was elated with how fun and creative they were! I was swept away with how well studied the chapters were, the rich questions she asked and the thought provoking statements she made! You are going to win if you pick up Believe ANYWAY and her other books! — **Amy Schafer** | Co-Pastor of Grace Life Church Pittsburgh, Pennsylvania | Co-Host "Hope Today" and "Sister-to-Sister"Cornerstone Television Network

Believe ANYWAY is the perfect followup book to Happy ANYWAY and Love ANYWAY! God has an amazing plan for our lives....one that includes being happy and worry-free because our trust is in Him. Adrienne makes believing God simple in the face of any and all circumstances. This is not just a book of concepts, but Adrienne has lived what she preaches! It will challenge you to Believe ANYWAY in every situation!
— **Pastor Janet Brazee** | World Outreach Church Tulsa, OK

WHERE DID ALL THIS HOPE TO BELIEVE ANYWAY COME FROM?

Hands down, without a doubt, when I am tempted to lose hope, give up, and throw in the towel, all I have to do is picture my beautiful three boys, Kevin, Gavin, and Garrison for just a split second, and all the inspiration, hope, and drive come rushing back to give me strength to sojourn on. Nothing and no one else in this universe spurs me on to be the best version of me possible than these three humans I adore. Guys, I love you more than you can ever begin to imagine.

I thank you for putting up with all of this happy...and battles I've fought to find it and keep it! Thank you for loving me ANYWAY when you've had a front row seat to see that I am not an expert at this, but rather have seen me fail my way forward as God works this all out in me more fully each day. Thank you for not losing hope in God and in each other in this fight of faith. I dedicate Believe ANYWAY to you because you each live this out so authentically. I am proud of our family for doing our utmost to navigate this thing called ministry. It has cut so deep, but it has also given us fun that few ever get to experience. It has been more meaningful than mortal souls are meant to even be able to handle - both good and bad. The low lows pale in comparison to the high highs we have been afforded. I pray that the words in this book will always be our anthem as a family first, and then after that, to my amazing readers and their families: Believe ANYWAY...no matter what life throws at you! God is Love is Happy.

Kevin, Gavin, and Garrison, this is the final book of this series and I am looking forward to some of the best times we have ever had together to celebrate this series being complete. Our next few years are going to be our best yet as a family, and as individuals as you boys launch into adulthood successfully. You have what it takes. Never doubt it. Believe ANYWAY in the face of adversity and don't shrink back. Always yield to your dad's kind nature and your mom's fierce tenacity. Most of all, to God inside of you, who has made you both so brilliant, creative, and brave, loving, strong, and faithful. World, look out, here they come! Babe, I could never have asked for a more romantic lover, a more engaged father for our boys, or a better leader of our family and ministry. Your support for my dreams means the world. Hey, now that these boys are out of the house, oh the love we have to share and the happy we have to enjoy! Thanks for believing in me ANYWAY, ya'll, no matter what I threw your way.

People are often unreasonable, irrational, and self-centered;

FORGIVE THEM ANYWAY.

If you are kind, people may accuse you of selfish, ulterior motives;

BE KIND ANYWAY.

If you are successful, you will win some false friends and some true enemies;

SUCCEED ANYWAY.

If you are honest and frank, people may cheat you;

BE HONEST AND FRANK ANYWAY.

What you spend years building, someone may destroy overnight;

BUILD ANYWAY.

If you find serenity and happiness, they may be jealous;

BE HAPPY ANYWAY.

The good you do today, people will often forget tomorrow;

DO GOOD ANYWAY.

Give the world the best you have, and it may never be enough;

GIVE THE WORLD THE BEST YOU HAVE ANYWAY.

You see, in the final analysis, it is between

YOU AND YOUR GOD.

It was never between you and them anyway.
— Mother Teresa (adapted by Adrienne Cooley)

Believe

Contents

"When everything was hopeless, Abraham believed anyway deciding to not live on the basis of what he saw he couldn't do but on what God said he would do."

Romans 4:18
The Message

Introduction:

This book was designed to fit like those perfect shoes in our closets that we can wear with shorts, jeans, or a skirt. My favorite books are the ones I can make notes in, the ones that make me ponder questions and rethink some of my faulty belief systems but aren't too complicated for me to comprehend. This book can be used as a private devotional, a small group curriculum, or a book-club option. Great news! The devotional could take only ten minutes on days when you're hurrying out the door, or you can sit and study for hours when you have the time. It was designed with both our busy lives and our hunger for more of God in mind. Each of our lives are custom-designed and unique in their own way. This book is meant to fit your lifestyle on each day, no matter what life throws at you. Customize it for your own purposes and use.

In Happy ANYWAY and Love ANYWAY, we learned that the secret to a happy and fulfilled life is love. In Believe ANYWAY, I want to share how to thrive in life through a faith that can move mountains. We will answer some big questions like…

How do you continue to believe when your answer doesn't appear the way you thought it would? Is it really true that if you can see it, then you can be it? Is it seriously possible to have the life you've always dreamed of, and if so, how? How do we pray prayers that get answered? Could our happiness, and the lack thereof, be connected to our ability to Believe ANYWAY? Why does our faith keep falling short?

"Happy are those who trust the Lord."
Psalm 40:4 GNB

This is our theme verse for the book. Have you ever noticed we are a whole lot happier when we are trusting the Lord? If you think about it, the last time you were really upset or worried about something, you probably were not fully trusting God, regardless of the state of your situation. This verse says it best. When we Believe ANYWAY, we thrive!

Each chapter has a section called "Don't Stop Believing," which challenges you to think about the goals you can have in each of the seven baskets of life. In this section, I will guide you through prayerfully setting these goals in the following areas: Spiritual, Personal, Family, Social, Financial, Career, and Health.

Each chapter also has a section called "The Science of Believing" and we will read about the actual science behind that week's devotion. My aim is that each chapter of this book will help you to thrive in life: spirit, soul, and body.

You are going to love using the H.O.P.E. method, along with all of the verses mentioned each week. The H.O.P.E. method of studying scripture is an acronym. The "H" stands for His Story, which is where you will write down a verse you want to further study from that week's lesson. The "O" stands for Observation. This is where you will write down what you observe as the Holy Spirit reveals things to you about that particular verse. "P" is for Prayer. Something about writing your prayer, regarding a specific verse, helps articulate what is in your heart. "E" is for Expectation. This is where you will be invited to visualize the scripture you wrote coming to pass in your life, writing what your expected outcome will be, according to your faith.

There are moving testimonies shared by incredible authors, influencers, and also ordinary people like you and me in each chapter. I know these stories will inspire you to Believe ANYWAY, trusting God to come through for you just like He did for these individuals!

Lastly, I hope you will enjoy all of the fantastic quotes, verses, and activity pages throughout. I added them just for the fun of it. I know you will get as much out of what you write, as out of what I wrote. I implore you: set aside time, not just to read this book, but to fully engage with it.

I can't wait to connect with you on social media, and hopefully see you at a Happy Girl Conference one day!

XOXO
ADRIENNE

SEE IT

&

BE IT

Believe

LET'S GET TO KNOW EACH OTHER A BIT...

As a little girl from rural America, I grew up with big dreams, a big imagination, and an even bigger God that I believed in with my whole heart. It was underneath Mississippi pines that I would sit and ponder what life could be like. I would ride my horse to the back of our thirteen-acre pasture and pray about my future. I would lay on a quilt in a field of weeds, that I thought were flowers, which flowed right up to the edge of our little pond. On many summer evenings, I would look up at the stars, imagining all kinds of places God would take me. I remember hours spent in my treehouse in the back left corner of our acreage, across the little stream that fed from our neighbor's pond into ours.

> I would cry out, "God, I know you have big plans for me. I surrender my life to you."

I would dream of flying all over the world, telling people about the Lord. I would pray for the gospel to be preached from the big screen and for Christian films to be produced. I prayed for my family members to be saved and daydreamed of God's blessings that would come to those who served Him. I remember many nights, as a tween, praying for God to be with my future husband and to keep him wherever he was in the world at that time. Little did I know that his parents were going through a divorce and he desperately needed my prayers in those very moments. I believe that although my life looked nothing like it looks now, my future was beginning to take shape through prayers of faith. I "saw" in my heart, way back then, so many things I have since been ever so blessed and honored to be able to live out.

Some of the greatest preachers of the day would come to our church and pray over me. Time and time again, they would speak of the call of God on my life. I was a "nobody" in our church. You know what I mean. Our family would not have been considered pillars of the church or really part of the "in clique." My mom was shy and a little self-conscious because my dad didn't go with her to church. He was a truck driver and gone most of the time. Now that I am a pastor's wife, I have extra respect for all the women who come to church alone, looking around at all the seemingly happy, perfect couples and wishing more than anything to have their husbands in the seat next to them. My mom didn't let that feeling keep her from packing up her three kids, and usually other friends of hers and ours, into our 70's conversion van, complete with the little round window and a purple sunburst paint job. She would haul us forty-five minutes to a church that was about two decades before its time and had a massive impact on my life. At fifteen, my precious youth pastors asked me to speak in "big church" and I preached my first sermon titled, "Compassion." I was so nervous on the way to church and the Holy Spirit convicted me then, warning me that being nervous was proof I was thinking of myself rather than the people He called me to minister to. To this day, the moment I get nervous before speaking or doing anything "big" for God, I remember that day, many moons ago, and do my best to take my thoughts off of myself and set my mind on Him and others. I'd like to do that right now.

Enough about me... what have you imagined and prayed for in your life that has or hasn't come to pass yet? Go onto my Facebook page and join my Facebook group. I'd love to hear from you and see what you are believing to get out of this study and get to know a little bit about you!

We all have things we are still believing for that have not happened yet. And this first week is going to put faith and courage into you so that you can

Believe ANYWAY, no matter how things look. I know you will be equipped through this study with The Word of God and with practical tools that are going to help you to live out the life you have always wanted. Such as I have, give I thee. I don't have a perfect life, but I do have a life that I love. I am super excited about the privilege to encourage you so that you can love your life, too! Maybe you already have a life you love and have figured all of this out. Well, we can all keep going from glory-to-glory together, right? Whether you are in a desperate situation or want to go from good to great, I pray this study will encourage you like it has me to **Believe ANYWAY**.

"For as {s}he thinks in her heart so is {s}he…"

Proverbs 23:7 (NKJ)

Believer

Have you ever noticed that when you are trying to get somewhere and call to ask directions, the first thing they ask is, "Where are you right now?"

Psalm 37:23 NLT says "The Lord directs the steps of the godly. He delights in every detail of their lives."

So let's start with where you are. Then you will know what steps are needed to get you where you want to be. I will be with you each step of the way, showing you how I went from discouraged, depressed, anxious, and defeated to filled with joy, love, and faith. The Lord will direct your steps and it tickles me pink to get to encourage you along the way.

What is your life like right now?

_____

_____

Describe your walk with God:

_____

_____

Describe your family life:

_____

_____

Describe your financial state:

_____

_____

Describe your career/grades:

_____

_____

Describe your physical fitness/health:

_____

_____

Describe your mental and emotional state:

_____

_____

Describe your personal development:

(What are you doing to better your skills and talents?)

_____

_____

Okay, so above is where you are. First you have to take a cold, hard look at reality (aka…where you are) before you can map out a vision for where you want to go.

Now we are going to do something really fun that will bring you out of the mulligrubs. Look to the horizon of where you could be if you will invest the time to finish this book, focusing on the practical applications for the next eight weeks. Are you ready to never be the same again?! I'm so excited because I know from experience that you are in for the ride of your life and you will never look back again! Let's do this!!

The power of seeing and believing in your heart is more real than what you see with your eyes. This world we live in - everything we see, feel, touch, smell, and hear - is a result of a world we cannot see. Don't be like Thomas in the Bible, "oh ye of little faith," having to see it with your eyes before you *believe* it.

Let's do a little exercise together and practice seeing with the eyes of your heart. The words below will become more than a wish list, as you add faith and genuine expectation.

> "Write the vision and make it plain on tablets that he may run who reads it."
> Habakkuk 2:2 NKJV

It has been proven that your goals are 42% more likely to be accomplished if you write them down.

Romans 4:17 says to call those things that be not as though they were. Let's do just that, have some fun and dream a little...or A LOT!

What would your life be like right now, if it were exactly how you want it to be?

Describe how you want your walk with God to be:

_____

_____

Describe how you want your family life to be:

_____

_____

Describe how you want your financial state to be:

_____

_____

Describe how you want your career/grades to be:

_____

_____

Describe how you want your physical fitness/health to be:

_____

_____

Describe how you want your mental and emotional state to be:

_____

_____

Describe your personal development: (What is a class, course, or book you can invest in to better your skills and talents?)

_____

_____

The Science of Believing:

Scientists have studied what actually happens to our brains when we imagine the things we desire. When we begin to focus on something we want, we notice that very thing everywhere. This is due to our Reticular Activating System (RAS) which creates a filter for what we focus on - good or bad. Our RAS goes to work, and we start seeing what we want.

CONFESSION TIME: When I was a little girl, I stayed with my cousin in the Mississippi Delta during the summer. My aunt had a Volkswagon bug convertible that she would cram us into and take us to the country club swimming pool while she played tennis. Imagine with me for a minute, a hot Mississippi day in the 70's. I'm sure I was in a halter top, maybe my favorite one with ruffles of pink, purple, yellow, and lime green polka dots. Oh, the fun I had, worlds away from where I lived. Those summer visits built a vision on the inside of me that led me to the lifestyle I enjoy today. Ever since then, I wanted a convertible. Twenty something years later, that is what I drive and anytime I need a day off and there isn't one in sight, I drop the top and am instantly on vacation. For the longest time, it was a pie-in-the-sky dream to own a convertible, but I wrote it down and made it a real goal. I placed it on my vision board. Guess what? It wasn't long before I had one.

Don't Stop Believing!

Think of a fulfilling life in terms of having different baskets that are all full of good things that bring joy and satisfaction. There are many different takes on this same concept, and you can see one version of this in the final chapter of my first book Happy ANYWAY. For our purposes, in this study, I'd like you to consider taking inventory of a specific basket or two of your life as you read each chapter of this book.

THE BASKETS OF LIFE ARE:

Spiritual	Personal	Family	Social	Financial	Career	Health

Tony Robbins says he has found that we all typically focus on only one or two of these. When I heard him say that, I thought, WOW! That explains so much. I immediately sat down and wrote them in the order of my priorities. Then I started thinking of friends who excel in various areas and wrote what I guessed their priorities were, based on what I saw of their lives. I quickly realized, AHA! The baskets of my life that are not as full are in direct correlation to the priority I have placed on that basket. It's as simple as that! So guess what this means? This is why the rich get richer. This is why _____ (you name the person) is succeeding in this area and not that one. It's because this is the basket they are focusing on, or not focusing on, with both passion and skill.

Great news for you and me!!!!! You are about to have the most balanced life ever because of this study. We are going to fill all the baskets with God's will, His Word, and His plan for our lives. No matter what you are going through right now, or what is keeping you from accomplishing your goals, we are going to get through this together. Ready, set, go!

For this chapter, let's look at the basket of Career. If you are a stay-at-home mom or wife, retired or otherwise not currently on a career path, this section still relates to you. Replace the word "career" with "purpose."

SET ONE CAREER GOAL TO BE ACCOMPLISHED:

1. in your lifetime   2. in five years

3. in one year   4. in three months

5. in one week

Write down something you are thankful for that has been accomplished already in this area. If you have a house, car, or eat three meals a day, those are things to be thankful for. Start with whatever you can be thankful for and don't sell yourself short. Sometimes it takes writing it down to see how far you have really come and how full your basket may already be. When I've done this, I have been like, "Whoa! I have so much to be thankful for." When you do this exercise, you will feel the same way and be encouraged to not give up, but instead, reach for the stars!

MY CAREER / SCHOOL / PURPOSE GOALS:

At the end of my life, I will have succeeded in my career if I accomplish

_____.

In five years, when I look back to this day _____

_____will have happened for me to be able to

say, "Yes! I did it!"

In one year, I will accomplish _____ at work/school.

In three months, these goals must be done in order to be on track for my
one year, five year, and lifetime goals to become reality:

_____

_____

This week I will make 3-5 tasks a priority because they are in line with what
God is showing me is His plan for my life. I will rise early and be diligent this
week to get these things done in order to reach my goals:

_____

for:_____

This is called total surrender. When we surrender to Him, we SEE what He
sees. THAT is when we start living the good life, able to BE who He has
called us to be! See it! Be it!

"dream it!
pin it!
live it!"

-Terri Savalle Foy

This is what we will call the H.O.P.E. process. It's the part of Believe ANYWAY where you will dig deeper into the scripture and mine out jewels that I believe God intends to speak to you in profound ways. Find the verses from this chapter that stand out most to you and put these verses through the **H.O.P.E. process.** The "H" stands for **His story.** Simply write out a verse from this chapter. The "O" stands for **Observation**. Ask God to show you what He wants you to observe from this verse the most. Write down what He speaks to you. The "P" stands for **Prayer.** Write out your prayer regarding this verse. What are you needing or wanting to see in your life? Ask Him for it. The "E" is for **Expectation** and this is where you will write out by faith, in present or past tense, what you expect to become reality in your life. Faith is now the substance of things hoped for and the evidence of things not yet seen as Hebrews tells us. This is where our hope turns into faith and brings things from the future into our present.

H IS STORY _____
_____

O BSERVATION _____
_____

P RAYER _____
_____

E XPECTATION _____
_____

H IS STORY

_____
_____
_____

O BSERVATION

_____
_____
_____

P RAYER

_____
_____
_____

E XPECTATION

_____
_____
_____

H IS STORY

_____

_____

_____

O BSERVATION

_____

_____

_____

P RAYER

_____

_____

_____

E XPECTATION

_____

_____

_____

H IS STORY

_____

_____

_____

O BSERVATION

_____

_____

_____

P RAYER

_____

_____

_____

E XPECTATION

_____

_____

_____

H IS STORY

_____

_____

_____

O BSERVATION

_____

_____

_____

P RAYER

_____

_____

_____

E XPECTATION

_____

_____

_____

See it & Be it!

CUT PICTURES OUT OF A MAGAZINE AND PLACE HERE FOR YOU TO SEE
IT AND BE IT. WRITES GOALS HERE AND DREAM BIG! WHY NOT?!

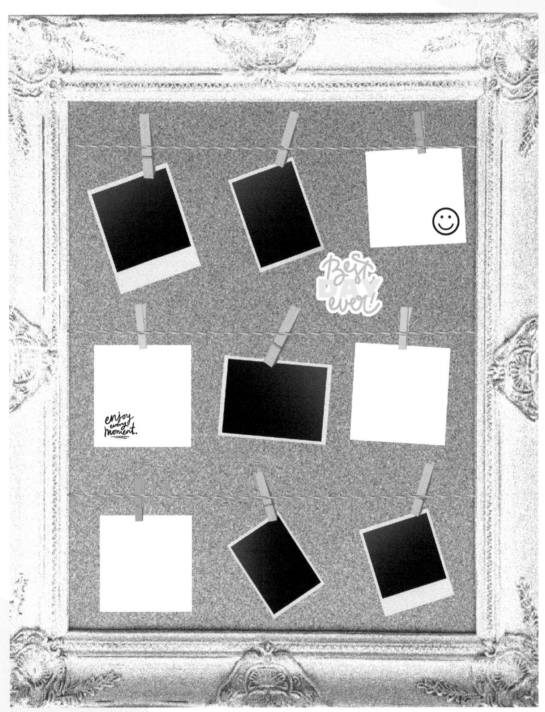

I Chose to Believe Anyway...

regarding losing weight and getting my dream house.
This is what happened...

"When I joined Harvest Church, led by Pastors Kevin and Adrienne Cooley, I had been battling for years with Hashimoto's Disease, which at my 5'4" frame had landed me at a hefty 198 lbs. Pastor Kevin preached a message on "...speaking things that be not as though they were..." according to Romans 4. I decided to acknowledge God, giving Him praise and thanks, first thing each morning, for what I knew He would do in my life.

The weight didn't come off immediately, but I didn't give up. Instead, I continued to pray to God daily. When I wanted God and my relationship with Him more than I wanted the weight loss, the weight fell off, 73 pounds worth!

A few years after this miracle of seeing and becoming thinner and healthier, I attended and served at the annual Happy Girl Conference that Adrienne hosts each year. Guest speaker, Terri Savelle Foy, introduced me to vision boards and the concept of seeing the vision and making it plain in a way I hadn't experienced before. I made long-term vision boards, short-term ones, and even a personal one just for my "forever" home.

The very next year we found it, barely looking, and everything fell into place. God has proven over and over, in these demonstrations within my life, that His word is truth and He is love! So, know that whatever you are believing Him for, nothing is too big for our God."

PAM WATTS

Happy Girl Conference Attendee,
Harvest Church Member, and friend

WEEK TWO

WHEN ALL
HOPE
IS LOST

Believe

WHEN YOU FEEL LIKE YOU CAN'T GET OUT OF BED...

When you don't know where your next mortgage payment is coming from...

When you failed royally and feel like it's over educationally for you...

When the pain is unbearable because of divorce, an affair, loss of a loved one, betrayal from a BFF, or losing your home to bankruptcy...

When you are torn between your divorced parents, or just broken because of your fractured family...

When you've gotten a diagnosis that promises very little hope in the prognosis...

When you have flipped your lid to the point of possible or actual insanity...

WHEN _____
(YOU FILL IN THE BLANK.)

Let's start with the most soothing, life-giving, hope-filled place we can, namely, scripture. When there has been devastating loss and our hearts feel shattered into a million pieces, the Word of God is like medicine.

I hope to care for you in this chapter to the best of my ability by ministering His Words of healing to you. He is the Great Counselor and Great Physician. I believe, as you connect your faith to the following verses, they will penetrate your mind, spirit, and body, giving you a sense of relief and hope regarding whatever you are facing right now. There are answers that we can find nowhere else except in His Word.

"Come to me, all you who are weary and burdened, and I will give you rest." **Matthew 11:28 NIV**

"For I know the plans I have for you,' declares the LORD, 'plans to prosper you and not to harm you, plans to give you hope and a future." **Jeremiah 29:11NIV**

"For I consider that the sufferings of this present time are not worthy to be compared with the glory which shall be revealed in us." **Romans 8:18 NASB**

"This hope is like a firm and steady anchor for our souls." **Hebrews 6:19, CEV**

If your loss is recent and you are in a vulnerable place, please pause here and ask the Holy Spirit to speak to you from one of these verses. Then journal your cry, His whispers, and any answers that come from letting these verses wash over your soul.

_____

_____

_____

_____

When I was dealing with loss one particular season, I read a book by Dr. Phil called, *Real Life: Preparing for the 7 Worst Days of Your Life*. It helped me sort through things in a healthier way than I had figured out how to do on my own. We all go through varying losses, handle them differently, and process them in healthy ways some days, and not-so-healthy ways other days. I highly recommend reading it if you have just come through a trage-dy. There are so many truths within this book.

ONE OF THE BIGGEST TAKEAWAYS I CAN SHARE IS THAT LOSS IS LOSS IS LOSS.

It is legitimate and valid to need to grieve whatever loss you have faced, whether a special person or a stolen purse. The Bible tells us that we perish for lack of knowledge. I strongly encourage you to get knowledge that will help you not to perish when you feel like that is exactly what you are doing. Grief can become so heavy that you cannot bear it if you don't gain knowl-edge about healthy ways to grieve. Read Hosea 4:6.

I have learned personally that dealing with loss is much like the feeling of waves that wash over you and make you feel like you may drown or be washed out to sea, emotionally, never to return. I've had others tell me it is like going into a box of grief to deal with emotions, cry, face the pain, and then come out of the box to go about life as best you can.

During the grief process, many therapists say it is healthy to "go into the box of grief." It's important, though, to learn your limit so you don't stay in too long or avoid facing things all together. Grief doesn't have to come in and take over your life. You can learn to ride the waves of grief, much like surfing. I picture the Word of God being like a surfboard that keeps us above the shark-infested waters heading us back to the stability of dry land.

If you have dealt with any kind of severe grief or tragedy, your heart is probably beating fast right now, as you are most likely tracking with every word. Or your heart may be soothed by these words because you relate and are learning to accept the new normal after loss.

Our responses to loss are as different as each one of us are from one to another. Something to remember when you feel like all hope is lost: All roads don't lead to Rome, but a whole lot of them do. In other words, overcoming hopelessness, grief, or loss can look very differently for each of us.

Describe how loss feels to you:

_____

_____

The common thread we all have, when finding our hope again, is that we begin to believe The Truth over what may be simply true. Truth trumps what is true.

For example, it may be true that this horrible thing has happened, but the greater Truth is that God will neither leave us nor forsake according to Hebrews 13:5. Proverbs 18:10 states that He is a strong tower, the righteous run into, and they are safe. The Truth is that with God nothing is impossible to those who believe, (Mark 9:23). There is mountain-moving faith inside of us if we are born again, (Mark 11:23). The Truth is that fear is a liar, (John 8:44). Greater is He that is in us than He that is in the world, (1 John 4:4). The Truth is that He supplies all our needs - spirit, soul, and body, (Philippians 4:19).

What may be true right now that could steal your hope, if you let it?

What is The Truth about your situation, according to His Word?

_____

_____

_____

During and after loss, there can be regret, shame, blame, hurt, pain, anger, hopelessness, lethargy, depression, and a level of loneliness that is unfathomable, along with a myriad of other emotions. This is a hard truth, but there is something else that we need to understand about loss. Pain will not kill you.

We were not promised that we would never have pain, but that Jesus bore our pain, grief, and sorrows. It's important to realize, though, that to be able to give our emotional pain to God, we first have to acknowledge it is there. We must face it and know that He is with us. We can always cast our cares upon Him. In His Presence is fullness of joy. We can go into His Presence sad, but come out of His Presence with joy, (Psalm 16:11b).

What is it that you need to bring into His Presence right now? What can you leave, so you can exit His Presence with the unfathomable JOY which is there for the taking?

As an act of faith, mark through the emotions that are weighing you down and that you need to leave at the altar in His Presence right now…regret, shame, blame, hurt, pain, anger, hopelessness, lethargy, depression, loneliness _____ _____ _____.

NOW, BY FAITH, CIRCLE WHAT YOU ARE TAKING FROM HIS PRESENCE! HINT: IT'S THE ONLY WORD TO CHOOSE FROM...

J O Y

....

I want to clear up a few things that a lot of Christians get hung up on.

- Our emotions are real and have to be dealt with, not ignored.

- Though our feelings will lie to us, the way to overcome them is to subject them to His Word and believe what God says over how we feel.

- It is not just okay to get help, but is scriptural to humble ourselves and ask for what we need. Sometimes our need is wise counsel. I am a huge proponent of Christian counseling, so much so, that at our Happy Girl Conference, I often have a mock therapy session with my therapist on stage. She also teaches in a workshop at the conference each year. You have not because you ask not, so ask someone who has the knowledge you need in order to get unstuck. We all get stuck at times and need a hand. Unashamedly reach out when you need it. The Bible tells us there is safety in the multitude of counselors, (Proverbs 11:14). Because of this Truth, I think we all need at least one! Get over yourself and go to counseling.

- Medicine is sometimes needed to stabilize a situation. If you were to endure a physical trauma requiring surgery, you would need anesthesia to get through the procedure, as well as physical therapy, in order to recover fully. Likewise, if you have sustained severe emotional trauma, you might need medical help to stabilize your mental health. There is no more shame involved in treating mental health than in taking medications to be able to endure surgery. Just as with our physical recovery, medicine isn't always enough. We need proper diet, healthy sleep habits, and sometimes physical therapy. Similarly, to complete our emotional healing, we need healthy relationships, lots of time in His Word, and sometimes therapy.

- What if you haven't experienced trauma, but find yourself in chronic pain or sadness? Some ongoing physical conditions require maintenance medicine. So do some mental illnesses and disorders. I am not a health professional and in no way giving medical advice. What I'm saying is: Don't ever think that taking medicine means you aren't in faith for your healing or that you are weak in some way. Believe God while taking it, that you will eventually not need it, if that is your desire. Treat it just like you would with any medicine you've taken for physical ailments. Usually, the underlying goal, when taking medicine, is to regain health, right? But while you need it, take it if it helps. The stigma that is associated with mental health is something I want to help remove. That is why I bring this up. I have met so many Christians who are ashamed of this topic. Shame takes us nowhere good! It takes us further away from where we are trying to go. Lose the shame and get help.

- Remember this: You always have a choice. When psychiatrists prescribe medicine to you, they tell you that it can help, but exercise and life choices also play a huge role. They all say this because you still have a choice and that is beautiful. Never surrender your choice to depression or anxiety or anything else. Science has proven that you can change your mood by simply making yourself smile, doing a jumping jack, or standing up straight and tall. You can make the choice of getting out of bed, even if only to put one foot in front of the other. You can choose to read the Word and build yourself up in order to beat the grief associated with loss. Or you can choose to let it beat you. Changing your physical state can change your mental state. Take this moment to think about how much changing your spiritual state could alter your mental state in positive ways.

"And do not be conformed to this world, but be transformed by the renewing of your mind, so that you may prove what the will of God is, that which is good and acceptable and perfect." **Romans 12:2 NAS**

When we renew our minds with His Word, it transforms us. It changes us from depressed to happy, from poor (in our minds) to thankful and from anxious to peaceful.

Loss can send our minds and emotions for a loop, to say the least. I asked my husband, "If you could only say a few sentences to someone who has lost all hope, what would you say?" This was his answer…

"EVERYTHING IS TEMPORARY. THIS IS NOT HIS PERFECT PLAN. COOPERATE WITH HIM AND HIS PRINCIPLES. THIS TOO SHALL PASS AND YOU WILL OVERCOME."

I should have known that is exactly what he would say. He says that to me all the time, even if I am in a frenzy over small losses or day-to-day challenges. Interestingly, it's sort of like swimming. Whether you are swimming in deep water or shallow water, it's the same. You're swimming.

Something I try to do is practice navigating the day-to-day things by confronting them with grace and faith, believing ANYWAY, no matter how things look. That's like swimming in shallow water, but it's still true. If we live a life of believing ANYWAY in facing the small things, when massive storms hit, we will walk on water and keep our eyes on Jesus, the Author and Finisher of our faith, because we have gotten into a habit of trusting Him in the small things. I have noticed that friends who weather major storms the best are the ones whose faith is strongly grounded in The Word. It's not that they are encountering no pain. They survive great pain successfully, while others flounder for years in despair and calamity.

The trials of life come to us all, but He is our strong tower and the righteous run into it and are safe. If you feel like life is beating you to smithereens, "RUN Forrest RUN" into His strong tower! You are safe there.

Go into His Presence, get real with God. He can handle it. You'll come out tasting and seeing that the Lord is good, filled with HOPE for a bright future! There is hope. It is never really lost…maybe misplaced momentarily. Find your hope in Him today and don't let the devil steal your tomorrow just because he stole your yesterday. Stop dwelling on the past. There is no future in it.

Find a scripture to stand on concerning your future. This is a great one:

> "For I know the thoughts that I think toward you, says the Lord, thoughts of peace and not of evil, to give you a future and a hope." **Jeremiah 29:11 NKJV.**

MAY I TELL YOU A STORY ABOUT WHEN I LOST MY MOM?

I was sitting in my living room weeping, which I did a lot that first year she was gone, and that's okay. I truly grieved. But one day I was just pitiful and kept talking about how sad I was. My husband said something very hard to hear, but it helped me break through that grief.

Kevin said, "Adrienne, I know you miss your mom, and we all do. I know it's different because you are her daughter, but if you don't start being thankful for those of us who are still here, some who want to love you, and are still here for you, they may not stick around a whole lot longer. She is gone and she isn't coming back. She would want you to enjoy those who are still here in your life."

He was in no way saying he wouldn't stick around. Of course, he would stay, but others who don't love me as unconditionally as he does might not. I made a choice that day to grieve less and begin to notice those who were still wanting to have coffee, go shopping, or simply call to chat. I began to celebrate all who surrounded me with support. I chose to become more thankful for the mom I had, instead of sad for the mom I lost.

A Small Tweak in Perspective Took Me to a Giant Peak!

What is a tiny tweak in your mindset that could take you to a giant peak in moving through grief, toward victory and joy?

_____

_____

"Under utterly hopeless circumstances {s}he hopefully believed"

Romans 4:18 (WNT)

Believer

There have been several times when all hope seemed to be gone in my life and I am sure you can think of times like this, too.

One such time was the summer between my junior and senior years in high school, just before my brother, Heath's, thirteenth birthday. We got the devastating news that he had leukemia. Our world stopped. It came to a screeching halt. Had we waited two more weeks before finding it, he would not have made it. Doctors told us he had a 50/50 chance of survival. Little did we know how drastically our lives, and especially Heath's, would change.

We encountered so many touch-and-go moments where he was completely fighting for his life. It was like we would take three steps forward and two steps back throughout his treatment. His blood count would get built up, only to plummet. He would overcome something he "wasn't supposed to be able to overcome" and then almost slip away.

Heath lost so much weight that it's hard to believe how he possibly recovered. Tears flood my eyes, even now, as I recall those images in my mind of his "skin and bone" arms and legs. Yet, tears of thankfulness also flow as I remember the faithfulness of God during those difficult days and years. I've tried to fathom all that little guy was going through.

Still, I only know my perspective as his big sister. As hard as it was for all of us, there is no comparison to what he withstood physically, spiritually, and emotionally to beat that horrible disease. He was such a great little football player. Everyone was already talking about his potential for college ball as a middle-schooler. He had the build, height, and skill, until this awful disease hit and left no chance for those dreams to ever come true.

However, Heath's sense of humor is among my first memories when I reflect back on his year or more spent in the hospital. He made the best of his entrance into adolescence, as he fought for his life every day. And while his friends were fighting for the very football team position that he would have had on the football team. He decided he would still be an athlete, so he had a putting green and a golf club brought to his hospital room. Any time he had the energy, he "golfed" in his room.

When Heath's white blood count was up enough, he went around to the younger children's rooms, making them all laugh with his perfect Donald Duck impersonations. The whole floor would beg for Donald Duck to come and see them.

He was always playing pranks on his nurses. The best was when he filled the brand-new, clean urinal with apple juice and drank it when the nurse came in. Yes, I know. Gross. But it was hilarious. He was barely alive physically, yet he was so full of life. His main aim was keeping everyone laughing around him. His attitude was that he would "for sure" recover. Our entire family was totally persuaded of this, choosing to believe ANYWAY around every corner and every setback when all hope seemed lost.

Praise God. Despite an emergency appendectomy, when his immunity was at its lowest, and the surgeons didn't expect him to make it out of surgery, he did! It was not an easy road, and actually still isn't always, but he recovered and has been in remission for over thirty years. Today Heath has a beautiful wife, two brilliantly talented kids, and owns several businesses.

I felt privileged to be his bone marrow donor because we were a perfect match. We have a closeness that is so special to me. He is a constant reminder of what it means to believe ANYWAY…even when all hope seems lost.

The Science of Believing:

When my brother, Heath, was in Egleston Hospital on Emory University's campus in Atlanta, GA prepping for his bone marrow transplant, I was there in strict isolation for a few months before the transplant. As mentioned earlier, I was lucky enough to have the honor of being his bone marrow donor. That is how it was done in the late 80's.

I remember being absolutely fascinated with the newly emerging science of "Laughter Therapy" while there. Egleston Hospital had a Laughter Therapy room that we would visit when we could. There were comic books laying on the coffee table, along with joke books. There were comedians on the TV and the room was an uplifting, yellow color. We always left there happier than when we arrived.

Research is showing us how the smile that creeps up, exploding into uncontrollable laughter, has many health benefits. Studies show that this kind of laughter relieves stress and pain, boosts our immunity, reduces blood pressure, and dumps feel-good chemicals into our brain that improve our moods and stimulates our minds, according to the The Huffington Post.

Washington's Sibley Memorial Hospital opened a Laugh Cafe in 2012 where senior citizens could tell jokes and laugh together. The Cancer Treatment Centers of America and Ochsner Center for Integrative Medicine, along with many others, are making space for this therapy by creating similar programs.

Gina, my closest friend, is a physical therapist and has done Home Health for many years. She has confirmed this science from her own experience and constantly tells me, "Adrienne, people only see eighty years of age and beyond if they do it on purpose." She tells of the difference she sees in the health of the elderly. She has noticed that people only see beyond eighty with the right attitude, and beyond a healthy eighty with proper diet and exercise.

So, laugh your way out of your hopeless situation every chance you get. Be positive. It could help you not only live longer, but live better. The science is there to support the Truth that when all hope is lost, laughter is good like a medicine…just like the Bible tells us. (Prov. 17:22)

Don't Stop Believing!

LET'S GET BACK TO THE BASKETS OF LIFE.

Spiritual	Personal	Family	Social	Financial	Career	Health

For this chapter, let's look at the basket of Personal Development, specifically your emotional, mental, and intellectual health.

MY PERSONAL DEVELOPMENT GOALS:

At the end of my life, people will describe me like this:

_____

_____

In five years, when I look back to this day

_____

will have happened for me to be able to say, "Yes! I did it! I am who I want to be emotionally, mentally, and intellectually."

In one year, I will have accomplished these goals that will improve me emotionally, mentally and intellectually:

_____

_____

Examples: gone to counseling, read books, taken an online course or attended group gatherings to improve myself regarding

_____.

In three months, these goals must be done in order to be on track for my one year, five year, and lifetime goals to become a reality:

_____

_____

This week, I will make 3-5 tasks a priority because they are in line with what I believe God is showing me is His plan for my life. I will rise early and be diligent this week to get these things done in order to reach my goals:

_____

_____

When I get discouraged, I will think of all the progress I have made and be thankful. These are a few things I am most thankful for at this time regarding my mental and emotional health:

_____

_____

FAITH SEES THE
Invisible
BELIEVES THE
Incredible
& RECEIVES THE
Impossible

Wayne Myers

This is what we will call the H.O.P.E. process. It's the part of Believe ANYWAY where you will dig deeper into the scripture and mine out jewels that I believe God intends to speak to you in profound ways. Find the verses from this chapter that stand out most to you and put these verses through the **H.O.P.E. process.** The "H" stands for **His story.** Simply write out a verse from this chapter. The "O" stands for **Observation**. Ask God to show you what He wants you to observe from this verse the most. Write down what He speaks to you. The "P" stands for **Prayer.** Write out your prayer regarding this verse. What are you needing or wanting to see in your life? Ask Him for it. The "E" is for **Expectation** and this is where you will write out by faith, in present or past tense, what you expect to become reality in your life. Faith is now the substance of things hoped for and the evidence of things not yet seen as Hebrews tells us. This is where our hope turns into faith and brings things from the future into our present.

H IS STORY

_____
_____

O BSERVATION

_____
_____

P RAYER

_____
_____

E XPECTATION

_____
_____

H IS STORY

_____

_____

_____

O BSERVATION

_____

_____

_____

P RAYER

_____

_____

_____

E XPECTATION

_____

_____

_____

H IS STORY

_____

_____

_____

O BSERVATION

_____

_____

_____

P RAYER

_____

_____

_____

E XPECTATION

_____

_____

_____

H IS STORY

_____
_____
_____

O BSERVATION

_____
_____
_____

P RAYER

_____
_____
_____

E XPECTATION

_____
_____
_____

H IS STORY

_____
_____
_____

O BSERVATION

_____
_____
_____

P RAYER

_____
_____
_____

E XPECTATION

_____
_____
_____

Think on things that are pure & lovely & of good report. Notice as you fill in each section, your gratitude rises, you have the ability to live in the now and plan for a hopeful future!

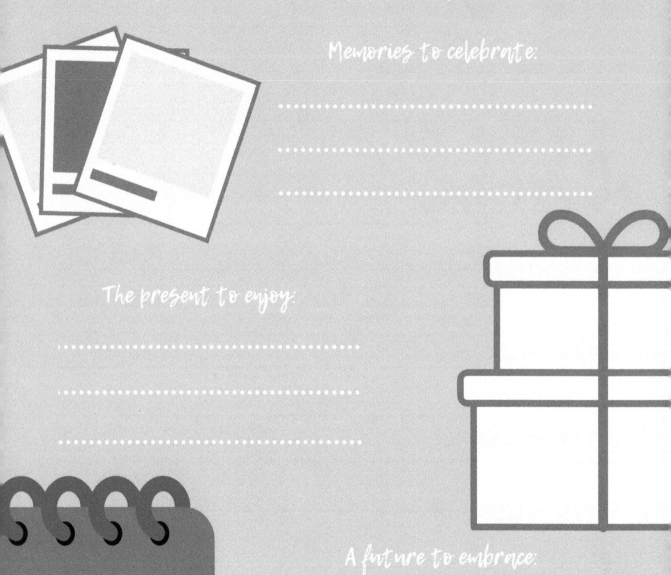

Memories to celebrate:

....

....

....

The present to enjoy:

....

....

....

A future to embrace:

....

....

....

I Chose to Believe Anyway...

in the midst of the greatest loss of my life and
this is what happened...

"I can remember the day when I got the phone call that left me completely lost - lost for words, lost about my future, and lost in my emotions. I was just shy of turning twenty, and I had been going to Rhema Bible College in Tulsa, Oklahoma. I was nearly one month from graduation. The phone call I received was from my grandmother who left me a voicemail saying that my father had just passed away from an unexpected heart attack at age forty-five.

To be honest, hope died on the day we buried my best friend, my dad. I was a daddy's girl who became suddenly overwhelmed within a giant sense of uncertainty.

Maybe you have lost something in your lifetime that was really valuable to you, like a wedding ring, or something a parent gave you as a child. Maybe, it was something more common like your car keys, your driver's license, your phone, or credit card. Maybe, you have experienced the loss of a job, a promotion, an opportunity, a marriage, a child, or a parent. It could be that you have lost your joy, your peace, or your zeal for life.

As a result of all the loss in your life, you've experienced a range of emotions: bitterness, anger, hurt, and disappointment. You've had regrets. Maybe you've given up on yourself and others.

You've quit believing in your dreams and goals, and found yourself saying, "The pressure of life is too great."

You may have even found yourself in a state where you quit believing, and that has led you to feel as if you have lost ALL HOPE.

I can honestly say that your hope isn't lost. It has just been mis-placed...temporarily. Deep down, we want to hope again, but we may not know how, or even where to start. Let me help you by telling you how I got my hope back! First, I had to realize that hope is a choice. It was MY CHOICE, and it's YOURS, too.

Hope is Not a Feeling, But a Decision.

You can choose to hope, or you can choose to quit. There is no middle ground. I found hope when I chose to find it. I had to make the decision. No one else could have made it for me.

Pastor Craig Groeschel once said, "Hope doesn't change a bad diagnosis, or unforeseen cir-cumstances, but it does CHANGE YOU."

A favorite scripture that has gotten me through the loss of my dad and other losses over the last twenty years is found in Hebrews 6:19-20 NASB: "This hope we have as an anchor of the soul, a hope both sure and steadfast and one which enters within the veil, 20 where Jesus has entered as a forerunner for us, having become a high priest forever accord-ing to the order of Melchizedek."

In the year 2015, the Lord spoke to me strongly about the call of God on my life and what I was to do with that calling. He told me it had everything to do with my name.

Well, growing up, I was not a fan of my name. I love the Lord's sense of humor! I had made up my mind that regardless of what I had lost, there was always hope for me when I CHOOSE it. Ever since then, any chance I get, whether from a pulpit or in a one-on-one conversation, I want to inspire others with the message of hope.

Here's the thing about loss. I would like to tell you that you will never have any kind of loss, pressure, or an unforeseen circumstance EVER again in your life. But you and I both know that is not the truth.

The truth is that we need to believe all of the Word of God and walk in all His promises. Don't use loss as an excuse. Once you hope in God in every circumstance, hope will be hard to stop.

At the end of the day, God is still God, and He is still Good."

HOPE LAMBERSON

Hope Lamberson communicates a message that inspires others to believe that, regardless of what they have lost, there is hope. Hope and her husband, Ryan, currently reside in Mississippi, with their three sons. You can find out more about her at hopelamberson.com

OUR

SECRET

WEAPON

WEEK
THREE

Believe

MUCH LIKE A POLICE OFFICER SHOWS HIS BADGE WHEN HE SHOUTS, "YOU'RE UNDER ARREST," WE HAVE A BADGE THAT IS BACKED UP WITH ALL OF THE POWER OF HEAVEN.

That badge is the Name of Jesus! We can whip out that badge every time the devil tries to pull one over on us and stop him in his tracks - if we only would.

The Name of Jesus carries with it all that He purchased with His Blood for us on the Cross. Jesus is our Savior - not only for eternal life, but also for this life on Earth - from sickness, disease, mental torment, and poverty.

Do I have your attention? Did you know this? It can sometimes be hard to believe ANYWAY when our circumstances don't line up experientially with the Word of God.

> "Surely, He has borne our griefs and carried our sorrows; Yet we esteemed Him stricken, Smitten by God, and afflicted. 5But He was wounded for our transgressions, He was bruised for our iniquities; The chastisement for our peace was upon Him, And by His stripes we are healed."
> **Isaiah 53:4-5, NKJV.**

Did you know that the word "chastisement" is defined as frustration? This means Jesus paid the price for the frustration of our peace. When we walk in anxiety and worry, we are not taking full advantage of what is ours through salvation. Isn't that great news?

When I learned this, it set me free from anxiety and worry. Of course, it's one thing to get free from something and another to stay free. Staying free comes from renewing our minds with His Word. Confession time: I have slipped back into some habits of worry even though the first chapter of Happy ANYWAY is: Don't Worry. Be Happy.

But writing this book has so filled me with faith that there has been a noticeable difference in my anxiety level. It has melted away because I've reminded myself of this revelation. Sometimes we have to put ourselves in remembrance of His Word, so that we can walk in the fullness of God.

Here is another passage to renew your mind which could, quite possibly, change your entire financial situation. Check this out!

> "For you know the grace of our Lord Jesus Christ, that though He was rich, yet for your sake He became poor, that you through His poverty might become rich." **2 Corinthians 8:9 NIV**

Note that this verse not only deals with finances. As such, it certainly includes money, money, money. Read down a few verses and it will become evident to you.

According to these verses, Jesus bore all of this so that we don't have to! Whoa! There would be so many doctors, bankruptcy lawyers, and therapists out of work if we chose to partake of what is rightfully ours as a result of the price Jesus paid for our whole salvation: Spirit, soul, and body.

Boomshackalacka!
Did that just fill your faith tank like it did mine?

If you want to fight for your right to be sick, broke, and defeated, go ahead. However, I am already busily taking hold of these verses for what they actually mean and using them to live the abundant life described in John 10:10.

> "The thief comes only in order to steal, kill, and destroy. I have come in order that you might have life--life in all its fullness." **John 10:10 GNT**

How differently would our lives be if we lived in understanding and agreement with this secret weapon? The secret weapon is the revelation knowledge of these truths.

The name of Jesus is sooooooo powerful! It's like we have a weapon in our hearts that is locked and loaded, waiting for us to pull the trigger. We can speak His Name above every name over any given circumstance and it absolutely must change. The Bible tells us in Romans 14:11, KJV "…For it is written, As I live, saith the Lord, every knee shall bow to me, and every tongue shall confess to God."

Sickness, poverty, anxiety and pain have to bow to His Name. Like we learned in the first week of this study from Proverbs 23:7, as we think in our hearts, so are we. Let's choose to see ourselves well, blessed, and thriving, no matter what life throws at us!

Okay, sounds great, right? But How? Prayer is how. Prayers that avail much are prayers filled with the revelation that everything must bow to His name and come into alignment with His Word.

Ephesians and Colossians prayers are great to pray often. If you have never prayed these prayers over your situation, your life is about to radically change! No doubt.

For years I prayed these prayers daily over my life. You can cover a lot of ground in prayer from these few passages. Go ahead and try it. Pray these prayers for yourself and for those you love. And as you do, please ask the Holy Spirit to guide you to use these prayers as a springboard, praying for all things that concern you. Get ready! Your prayer life is never going to be the same.

"For this reason I too, having heard of the faith in the Lord Jesus which exists among you and your love for all the saints, 16do not cease giving thanks for you, while making mention of you in my prayers; 17that the God of our Lord Jesus Christ, the Father of glory, may give to you a spirit of wisdom and of revelation in the knowledge of Him. 18I pray that the eyes of your heart may be enlightened, so that you will know what is the hope of His calling, what are the riches of the glory of His inheritance in the saints, 19and what is the surpassing greatness of His power toward us who believe. These are in accordance with the working of the strength of His might 20which He brought about in Christ, when He raised Him from the dead and seated Him at His right hand in the heavenly places, 21far above all rule and authority and power and dominion, and every name that is named, not only in this age but also in the one to come. 22And He put all things in subjection under His feet, and gave Him as head over all things to the church, 23which is His body, the fullness of Him who fills all in all." **Ephesians 1:15-23, NASB.**

"For this reason I bow my knees before the Father, 15from whom every family in heaven and on earth derives its name, 16that He would grant you, according to the riches of His glory, to be strengthened with power through His Spirit in the inner man, 17so that Christ may dwell in your hearts through faith; and that you, being rooted and grounded in love, 18may be able to comprehend with all the saints what is the breadth and length and height and depth, 19and to know the love of Christ which surpasses knowledge, that you may be filled up to all the fullness of God. 20Now to Him who is able to do far more abundantly beyond all that we ask or think, according to the power that works within us, 21to Him be the glory in the church and in Christ Jesus to all generations forever and ever. Amen." **Ephesians 3:14-21, NASB.**

"We give thanks to God, the Father of our Lord Jesus Christ, praying always for you, 4since we heard of your faith in Christ Jesus and the love which you have for all the saints; 5because of the hope laid up for you in heaven, of which you previously heard in the word of truth, the gospel 6which has come to you, just as in all the world also it is constantly bearing fruit and increasing, even as it has been doing in you also since the day you heard of it and understood the grace of God in truth; 7just as you learned it from Epaphras, our beloved fellow bond-servant, who is a faithful servant of Christ on our behalf, 8and he also informed us of your love in the Spirit." **Ephesians 1:3-8, NASB.**

Now it gets even better!

> "For this reason also, since the day we heard of it, we have not ceased to pray for you and to ask that you may be filled with the knowledge of His will in all spiritual wisdom and understanding, 10so that you will walk in a manner worthy of the Lord, to please Him in all respects, bearing fruit in every good work and increasing in the knowledge of God; 11strengthened with all power, according to His glorious might, for the attaining of all steadfastness and patience; joyously 12giving thanks to the Father, who has qualified us to share in the inheritance of the saints in Light."
> **Colossians 1:3-12, NASB.**

To recap, the secret sauce to believing ANYWAY is understanding that Jesus came to be our eternal salvation, which includes from now until forever. The revelation of what that fully means translates into us walking in all that God has provided for us. And when we use our secret weapon, the kind of prayer life described in this chapter, we become unstoppable by the enemy!

"The effective, fervent prayer of a righteous {wo}man avails much"

James 5:16b (NKJV)

Believe

"You treat me to a feast, while my enemies watch. You honor me as your guest,
and you fill my cup until it overflows."
Psalm 23:5, CEV.

I love the picture I get in my head when I think of this verse. It is an image I have had since I was a little girl. I see myself pulled up to a banquet table, with Jesus and the people I love. We are laughing and having a good ole' time, while our enemies are off just a little ways, watching and wishing they could get to us. But they can't. They can only watch and want to experience our good time and abundance.

This chapter would not be complete if I didn't share a couple of stories that will surely inspire your faith.

My mom attended a Bible study with several women in the late 1970's through the early 1980's. They had been studying about God's protection and the power of prayer. One evening, as one of the ladies was leaving, there was a guy waiting at the car to kidnap her, steal her car or do her some other kind of harm.

She just yelled, "Feathers, feathers, feathers in Jesus' Name!"

The verse they had been studying was Psalm 91:4 NIV, "He will cover you with His feathers, and under His wings you will find refuge; His faithfulness will be your shield and rampart." The guy took off (and maybe thought she was absolutely crazy). But hey, whatever works! She was a new believer and was quoting whatever part of the verse she could remember, adding her faith to it.

When we pray the Word, it's okay if all we can get out is "Feathers, feathers, feathers! in the powerful Name of Jesus!" He can work with that. We can still bank on His protection.

I think of the time when my husband hit a signpost in a parking lot a couple of weeks before our wedding, and my head went through the windshield. I was rushed to the emergency room in an ambulance. Blood was everywhere. Glass was in my eyes. It was very painful. I remember all I could do was speak the Name of Jesus. When I did, the pain would subside. It was amazing. I remember it like yesterday. I believed, with every ounce in me, that there was power in His Name and that Christ bore my pain. As I spoke His Name, the pain went away.

And yes, I know you were wondering. There are no scars, no lasting damage to speak of, and most importantly, my face was completely intact for the wedding.

The Science of Believing:

In a study conducted by the NYU Langone Medical Center, members of Alcoholic Anonymous were placed in an MRI scanner and shown drinking-related images to stimulate cravings. Yes, it sounds cruel, but it worked because they also learned the cravings were soon reduced when the participants - you guessed it - prayed!

The MRI data showed changes in parts of the prefrontal cortex, which is responsible for the control of emotion and the semantic reappraisal of emotion. The idea is that prayer gets us away from the fight or flight mode and can actually change our brain function and habits over time. It's scientifically proven. The interesting fact to note here is that, during prayer, the reflective regions of the brain are activated while the parts of the brain associated with action are inactivated.

I think of verses like, "Enter His courts with thanksgiving in your heart. Enter His courts with praise…"I remind myself of God's faithfulness in prayer. This then builds faith to **believe ANYWAY** in the face of any current situation.

I think it is so cool that, during prayer, the part of our brain associated with action is deactivated.

Could it be because our minds slow down enough to realize it is not us who is able to fix our problems, but Him? As we exalt Him above every problem we can rest in knowing He is the only way it is going to work out. Letting go and letting God releases the Holy Spirit to display the finished work of Jesus.

What does this mean? During times of stress, our nervous system becomes hyper-activated and goes into survival mode. This shuts down our executive functioning and prevents us from thinking clearly. Have you ever said something like, "I just can't think straight!" or "My head is spinning!"

Deliberately choosing to sit down and pray will help you regain control.

Something else happens when we pray. Prayer and meditation trigger the release of "happy chemicals" within the brain. According to Dr. Loretta Breuning, author of "The Science of Positivity" and "Habits of a Happy Brain," when we pray, we literally activate neural pathways we developed as children to release feel-good hormones such as oxytocin.

I found a remarkable article on nbcnews.com by Nicole Spector dated Feb. 16, 2018 1:02 pm. It is called, "This is your brain on prayer and meditation."

When my boys were babies and cried in the night or at nap time, I would go through a sort of checklist ritual. Feed them if they may be hungry. Change their diapers. Check their temperature. That was a couple of decades ago, so there may have been a few more things I don't recall, but you get the picture.

Once I knew all their physical needs were cared for, I would break into song to soothe them with "Jesus, Jesus, Jeeeeeeeeesus, There's just something about that name. Master, Savior, Jeeeeeesus, like the fragrance after the raaaaaain…." That song worked with Garrison and settled him every time. For Gavin it was, "Surely, the presence of The Lord is in this place. I can feel His mighty power and His graaaaaaace. I can feel the brush of angels wings…."

Those were songs of prayer that invited the Presence and power of God into the room and changed the atmosphere. Now I believe they even may have changed our brains, as science now suggests, so that I was able to calm the boys and get them to go to sleep. I believe we can apply these same principles and practices to be able to sleep or de-stress and deal rationally with mountains we are up against.

Don't Stop Believing!

Spiritual	Personal	Family	Social	Financial	Career	Health

For this chapter, let's look at the basket of your family and see what your goals are. Whether you are single or married without kids, with kids, or if you live at home with parents, you can do this exercise.

The greatest thing you can do for your family is pray for them just as this chapter has been talking about! We, as a family, like to set goals. We have even "checked" each other to see what we need from each other, maybe to change or make a request. One year, when our boys were young, they requested I not yell at them so much in the upcoming year. Yikes! True story. And I asked that they keep their rooms cleaner. LOL. It's okay. We also cheered each other on in the areas in which we were winning.

What are some things you want to see happen within your family?

MY FAMILY GOALS:

At the end of my life, I will have succeeded in my family if I accomplish

_____

_____

In five years, when I look back to this day

_____

_____

will have happened for me to be able to say, "Yes! I did it! I have a wonderful fulfilling family life."

In a year from now, I will:

_____

(Examples: be married, have been on a family vacation to ???, have my three year old potty trained, my thirteen year old in a certain school, my sixteen-year-old's car bought with cash, my college graduate launched into life and ready to thrive or be in a healthy place, one way or another, with my kids, parents or siblings.)

In three months, these goals must be done in order to

be on track for my one year, five year, and lifetime goals to become a reality:

_____

_____

(Example: will get our family on a routine and have meals together at least 3-4 times per week)

This week I will make 3-5 tasks a priority because they are in line with what I believe God is showing me is His plan for my life. I will rise early and be diligent this week to get these things done in order to reach my goals:

_____

_____

(Example: organize a closet, meal prep this weekend, call my parent, or have a quick family devotion each morning over breakfast)

When I get discouraged, I will think of all that I have to be thankful for when it comes to my family dynamic. These are a few things I am most thankful for:

_____

_____

GET YOUR

YOUR

KEVIN COOLEY

ASK

IN

GEAR!

This is what we will call the H.O.P.E. process. It's the part of Believe ANYWAY where you will dig deeper into the scripture and mine out jewels that I believe God intends to speak to you in profound ways. Find the verses from this chapter that stand out most to you and put these verses through the **H.O.P.E. process.** The "H" stands for **His story.** Simply write out a verse from this chapter. The "O" stands for **Observation**. Ask God to show you what He wants you to observe from this verse the most. Write down what He speaks to you. The "P" stands for **Prayer.** Write out your prayer regarding this verse. What are you needing or wanting to see in your life? Ask Him for it. The "E" is for **Expectation** and this is where you will write out by faith, in present or past tense, what you expect to become reality in your life. Faith is now the substance of things hoped for and the evidence of things not yet seen as Hebrews tells us. This is where our hope turns into faith and brings things from the future into our present.

H IS STORY
_____
_____

O BSERVATION
_____
_____

P RAYER
_____
_____

E XPECTATION
_____
_____

H IS STORY

_____
_____
_____
_____

O BSERVATION

_____
_____
_____
_____

P RAYER

_____
_____
_____
_____

E XPECTATION

_____
_____
_____
_____

H IS STORY

_____

_____

_____

O BSERVATION

_____

_____

_____

P RAYER

_____

_____

_____

E XPECTATION

_____

_____

_____

H IS STORY

_____

_____

_____

O BSERVATION

_____

_____

_____

P RAYER

_____

_____

_____

E XPECTATION

_____

_____

_____

H IS STORY

_____

_____

_____

O BSERVATION

_____

_____

_____

P RAYER

_____

_____

_____

E XPECTATION

_____

_____

_____

This is ME! Fill in each blank with what
redeemed thought or scripture you will "put on"
each day in order to win your current battle.
(Read Colossians 3 & Galatians 6)

umbrella (helmet) of salvation

Bible (sword)
of the Spirit

purse (shield)
of faith

God's-Girl belt of truth

Dress
(breastplate)
of righteousness

high heel (boots)
of peace

I Chose to Believe Anyway...

and this is what happened...

From the depth of my being I cried, "Lord, teach me to pray." Our first born and only son was addicted to drugs. My husband and I were preparing for David's college career and his three sisters adored their big brother.

Early one morning, my expectancy level was high as I sat at my kitchen table with Bible, paper and pen. I read, " Now this is the confidence that we have in Him, that if we ask anything according to His will, He hears us. And if we know that He hears us, whatever we ask, we know that we have the petitions that we have asked of Him." (1 John 5:14-15)

Staring at that scripture I asked the Holy Spirit, "How do I draft a petition that I could present to my Father?" A petition? I had never heard of such a thing! A few hours later a neighbor knocked on my door with a petition to the governor of our state! I asked her about the fundamentals of writing a petition. I had my answer.

When she left, I hurried back to find out what God said about children. "All your children shall be taught by the Lord, And great shall be the peace of your children. In righteousness you shall be established; You shall be far from oppression, for you shall not fear; And from terror, for it shall not come near you." (Isaiah 54:13-14)

I replaced "And all your children shall be disciples" with "David is a disciple taught by the Lord." Theology tried to tell me I was misusing this scripture, but I knew this was a word from the Spirit of God to me.

My Father revealed David's true identity; he was a disciple! David's behavior did not define him. When others complained about something he did or said, my standard answer was, "I understand why you are upset with him. That's not who he is on the inside." God had opened my blind eyes and I saw God's creation and knew that he had a divine destiny, and I believed anyway.

My secret weapon became scriptural prayers. Through encouragement and discouragement, it was God's Word that anchored me to **Believe Anyway!**

(Today, David is the business manager and Vice President of Prayers That Avail Much. You can order a video of his testimony at www.prayers.org)

GERMAINE COPELAND

New York Times Best Selling Author
Prayers That Avail Much

Germaine Griffin Copeland, founder and president of Word Ministries, Inc., is the author of the Prayers That Avail Much family of books. Her writings provide scriptural prayer instruction to help you pray more effectively for those things that concern you and your family and for other prayer assignments. Her teachings on prayer, the personal growth on the intercessor, emotional healing and related subjects have brought understanding, hope, healing, and liberty to the discouraged and emotionally wounded. She is a woman of prayer and praise whose highest form of worship is the study of God's Word. Her greatest desire is to know God. Germaine is the daughter of the late Reverend A.H. "Buck" and Donnis Brock Griffin. She and her husband, Everette, have four children, and their prayer assignments increase as grandchildren and great-grandchildren are born. Germaine and Everette reside in Roswell, a suburb of Atlanta, Georgia.

CRAZY FAITH

WEEK FOUR

Believer

WHEN I THINK OF CRAZY FAITH, I THINK OF...

- When Jesus fed the ten thousand with a fish snack and a few pieces of bread.

- When Peter walked on water.

- Daniel in the lion's den.

- Shadrach, Meshach, and that other guy.

- Joseph and the coat of many colors.

- David and Goliath.

- The woman with the issue of blood.

- The woman at the well.

- The stories of Esther and Ruth.

- Mary washing Jesus' feet and going to great expense to do so.

- The time a precious little boy's finger grew out, right before our eyes, after we prayed for him in Arizona.

- Countless miracles of healing from Malaria in Calcutta

- The time my husband felt led to declare a fast and not eat the food prepared for him and his team in a village in India, after walking for hours to get there. They were all very hungry and tired, only to find out their food had been poisoned. When the village chief heard that the One true living God told Kevin to fast and pray for their village, he knew God was real and he made Jesus the Lord of his life and was saved. We planted a church in that village and preached the gospel to the whole village.

- The time when Kevin was held at gun point in Jackson, MS after preaching in an inner-city park as a teenager. Kevin told the guy to pull the trigger (and that he knew where he was going) and asked, "Do you know where you are going?" To which the gang member replied, "You're crazy, white boy!" and took off running away from him.

- The time Kevin saw a basketball-sized tumor shrink in front of his eyes in a village outside of Nagpur when he was nineteen. The result was a woman who was left completely whole.

- The time a tumor fell off in our Bible School student's hands in Bangalore when they prayed for a lady outside of a hospital.

- The time in India when Gavin and I were coming home from grocery shopping and something inside said to put Gavin, then a toddler, in my lap and a moment later, a car rammed into the door and hit us from the side where Gavin had been sitting only a second earlier. There were no seatbelts there. We were in the backseat, being driven. God is so good!

- The time when angry, loud men shouted at me in Hindi, while trying to break into our flat in Calcutta. They screamed, "I want the baby!" It was my strength against theirs, two grown men. I yelled for Kevin to come and help. He distracted them and we slammed the door and put the bar across it (which was the only way we had to lock it). We found out later, that at that exact time, a family member was praying and leaning against her bed post saying, "No, in Jesus' name, no! You may not!" There was no way except with supernatural help, that I could have kept them out, and I am convinced it was from those prayers filled with crazy faith that kept them causing whatever harm they were attempting.

- The time when we were youth pastors and a teenager in our group tried to take her own life. As we prayed over her at the hospital in ICU, the machines that were hooked up to her went crazy.

  The doctors came in asking, "What did you do?"

  We replied, "Nothing, but God is healing her."

  Shortly afterward, she became stable. Glory to God! She is a counselor today, thriving in her walk with God.

- When families in our church were put back together because dozens of couples decided to yield to faith that works by love instead of divorce.

- When a family once decided to start tithing by faith, and soon after, got a 10% increase promotion.

- When I chose to believe God in the midst of my battle with depression and take Him at His Word. He changed my name to "The Happy Lady"!

You serve the same God I serve, and that my husband serves, and all of those people in the Bible and the folks I wrote of in these stories!

You know what CRAZY FAITH is?

It is faith the size of a mustard seed that we can decide to yield to and get crazy enough to believe ANYWAY no matter what. We crazily believe that the Word of God is true and that His love for us is huge. That's crazy faith! It's not about us or the measure of the miracle that happens in our lives. It's about God's amazing love expressed through His power that corrects things in our lives.

"The Lord will accomplish that which concerns me." **Psalm 138:8a NASB**

What needs to be perfected in your life (big or small) that feels like you need crazy faith to get through?

_____

_____

Guess what? You have just enough faith for whatever you need. Simply believe ANYWAY, and watch Him turn your situation around. The Bible tells us we have all been given a measure of faith. But the Bible also says, "But be doers of the word, and not hearers only, deceiving yourselves." James 1:22 NKJV

In what way could you begin being a doer of the Word that could change your situation, or the situation of another? Is God leading you to be bold and share your faith more? Is He leading you to start a business and act on faith to do it? Is He calling you to ministry? Is He saying to change your diet, or to exercise? What is God leading you to DO, in line with His Word, that may take crazy faith, but you know, if you did it, would radically change your life or the life of someone else?

_____

_____

These are some key verses you need to let soak into the deepest part of the core of who you are if you want to live a life of crazy faith. I double-dog-dare you to look these up, dwell on them, memorize them, declare them, and watch them carry you to the other side - time and time again!

Mark 11:23-25
Mark 16:15-18
Matt 19:26
2 Corinthians 4:7-18
Philippians 4:13
Romans 8:37

There are so many more! What verses inspire you most to have crazy faith?

_____

_____

IDEA: Write a go-to Crazy Faith verse out on a notecard and keep it in your purse to pull out when you are stressing, or just need to feed your faith.

Here's a good one you could write out and keep with you!

"But seek first the kingdom of God and His righteousness, and all these things shall be added to you." **Matthew 6:33 NKJV**

Isn't it cool how, after this devotion, you feel like you can take on the whole world?! It's because faith comes by hearing, and hearing by the Word of God according to Romans 10:17. You know what's even cooler? You CAN take on whatever life throws at you. God will never allow you to come up against anything that he won't also provide for you the way of escape. (Read 1 Corinthians 10:13)

⁴ You are of God, little children, and have overcome them, because He who is in you is greater than he who is in the world.

The Science of Believing:

We previously discussed the scientific proof about how anxiety and other emotional and mental health challenges can affect us physically, manifesting in all sorts of ways, while even leading to disease. What about when anxiety is caused by a physical problem like thyroid dysfunction?

How often are we trying so hard (spiritually and mentally) to overcome what we may not be aware of as a physical health problem? Then what? Far too often we ignorantly shame ourselves and others in ways we would never shame someone else if they had a broken leg, instead of a mental or emotional issue.

It is really important for us to understand that it's difficult at times to separate the three: spirit, soul, and body. We must care for all three parts of ourselves because each one affects, and is impacted, by the other. We aren't always sure which is affecting which. If we "chase the wrong rabbit," we come up short and fail to thrive.

CONSIDER THESE FACTS BELOW WHEN YOU AREN'T SURE IF YOUR PHYSICAL AILMENT IS STRESS-RELATED, OR IF YOUR STRESS IS DISEASE-RELATED.

According to the Cleveland Clinic, anxiety could be brought on by both over the counter and prescription drugs, herbal supplements, homeopathic remedies and food additives (particularly MSG); too many energy drinks or coffee. Other emotional issues may flow from thyroid, parathyroid, and adrenal conditions. Some suffer without knowing the cause may be an infectious issue such as Lyme Disease. Other upsets may flow from vitamin deficiencies/overload. Electrolyte abnormalities and environmental toxins can bring injury to the central nervous system, along with brain tumors, and other diseases.

Later on, take a look at this link:

https://health.clevelandclinic.org/is-a-hidden-medical-condition-causing-your-anxiety/

The point here is to be sure what you are facing isn't physical, while you're busily dismissing it as an emotional or spiritual issue. Love yourself enough to find out which part of you may need a littleTLC and attention.

Your spiritual, mental, and physical health are all necessary for you to thrive. The good news is The Great Physician is a specialist in all three areas. At the end of the day, or better yet in the beginning of the day, go to Him and allow Him to guide you toward healing. Nothing is too big for Him!

Don't Stop Believing!

Spiritual	Personal	Family	Social	Financial	Career	Health

For this chapter, let's look at the basket of Health.

Miracles such as we discussed, are a great thing. I'm so thankful for all of the amazing miracles we have seen in our lives, and for what you've experienced too. Yet, God's greatest desire for us, because of His great love for us, is to walk in the abundant life, instead of having to go from miracle-to-miracle. This Truth applies to our health.

Our bodies were not designed to live with stress, fear, or depression running through our veins 24/7. Our bodies were designed to live with peace, love, and joy permeating throughout us, day and night.

I talked about this a lot more in my previous two books Happy ANYWAY and Love ANYWAY. I strongly encourage you to get those books, or if you have them, get them back out and go through them. This is especially true if you find yourself having psychosomatic symptoms like headaches, IBS, fibromyalgia, GERD, or unexplained aches and pains.

Let me clarify, once again, that I am not a medical professional. I am in no way giving medical advice; however, science has certainly discovered a link between these symptoms and stress, anxiety, and depression. So, a little extra happy and love sure won't hurt!

What are some health goals you have? I am believing with you to walk in divine health. Sometimes part of walking in divine health is listening to what the Holy Spirit is leading us to do in this area. Let the Holy Spirit guide you in creating these goals and trust Him to help you walk them out. Let's do this...

MY HEALTH AND FITNESS GOALS:

At the end of my life, I will have lived a healthy and fit life if I accomplish living until _____years of age. A life of health and fitness to me looks like

_____.

In five years, when I look back to this day

_____

will have happened for me to be able to say, "Yes! I did it! I am in great health."

In one year, I will weigh _____ lbs. and be free from all disease. My other health and fitness goals for one year from now are:

_____

_____

In three months, these goals must be done in order to be on track for my one year, five year, and lifetime goals to become a reality:

_____

_____

This week I will make 3-5 tasks a priority because they are in line with what I believe God is showing me to be His plan for my life. I will rise early and be diligent this week to get these things done in order to reach my goals:

_____

_____

(Example: wake up at _____. Go to the gym _____ days for ___minutes/hr. Eat a clean diet. I will cut out_____.)

When I get discouraged, I will think of all that I have to be thankful for when it comes to my health. These are a few things I am most thankful for:

_____

_____

If a man can predict his own death and **resurrection**, and pull it off, I just go with whatever that man says.

ANDY STANLEY

This is what we will call the H.O.P.E. process. It's the part of Believe ANYWAY where you will dig deeper into the scripture and mine out jewels that I believe God intends to speak to you in profound ways. Find the verses from this chapter that stand out most to you and put these verses through the **H.O.P.E. process.** The "H" stands for **His story.** Simply write out a verse from this chapter. The "O" stands for **Observation**. Ask God to show you what He wants you to observe from this verse the most. Write down what He speaks to you. The "P" stands for **Prayer.** Write out your prayer regarding this verse. What are you needing or wanting to see in your life? Ask Him for it. The "E" is for **Expectation** and this is where you will write out by faith, in present or past tense, what you expect to become reality in your life. Faith is now the substance of things hoped for and the evidence of things not yet seen as Hebrews tells us. This is where our hope turns into faith and brings things from the future into our present.

H IS STORY _____
_____

O BSERVATION _____
_____

P RAYER _____
_____

E XPECTATION _____
_____

H IS STORY

_____

_____

_____

O BSERVATION

_____

_____

_____

P RAYER

_____

_____

_____

E XPECTATION

_____

_____

_____

H IS STORY

_____

_____

_____

O BSERVATION

_____

_____

_____

P RAYER

_____

_____

_____

E XPECTATION

_____

_____

_____

H IS STORY

_____

_____

_____

O BSERVATION

_____

_____

_____

P RAYER

_____

_____

_____

E XPECTATION

_____

_____

_____

H IS STORY

_____

_____

_____

O BSERVATION

_____

_____

_____

P RAYER

_____

_____

_____

E XPECTATION

_____

_____

_____

Believe Anyway Word Find

```
              V V X G W U
              Y T Z D O S
              M E T W B U
              S V M T E V
              A E U B Y O
              S I T I F R
              S Q B T C Z
D K E I U R C X N C D S P O P Y O N U N
Z H F R A U S Z O A Y V F S X P Y P X T
E C Q T U D M I R A C L E N U I T M P F
K E U Z V T I J M J T H Y E E S E I P U
A N Y W A Y U I I C Y Q V R N I E E J R
B S Z J M U N F C Q E E V X A G H J S H
              S B F I N A
              Y E L P L S
              N E Q T V J
              B H T I A F
              T I P R Z E
              P B Z D N Y
              P T F R N D
              L R A A P X
              Y E A I Z P
              G H H Y M H
              W B S E E L
              F B X E I R
              F C Q R W D
              E E N I O A
              V C Q N N Y
              O B N W A D
              L V X K I R
              M L O K B Z
              H U E R Z J
              L T P G J P
              B S M A W W
              E U U T F N
              P R V B X Q
              O T T G C A
              H H N E G P
              X M D Y A M
```

WORD LIST:

ANYWAY	FUTURE	LOVE	PRAYER
BELIEVE	HOPE	MIRACLE	SEE
FAITH	JESUS	OBEY	TRUST

109

I Chose to Believe Anyway...

and this is what happened...

I couldn't have expected in my wildest dreams what was going to happen that day. It all seemed so ordinary.

The routine was set. Get up. Pray. Get ready. Go to the cafeteria for breakfast. Head to class. Bible school. A girl like me shouldn't have even been admitted to Bible school. I had only been born again a few years and was clueless honestly on how things worked in Christendom. I didn't know I should wear a slip under my skirt – heck, outside of my gaberdine school uniform I never wore skirts. Even the color bra under my white blouse was a mystery; wear black, white, beige? Who knew? I didn't. So, I got in trouble over and over for ignorant inappropriate behavior and attitudes. Spending almost two years on probation seemed to validate that

thought, I don't belong here. Yet, I pushed passed that to answer the call of God on my life.

In the bubble of worship, praying students, courses on the Holy Spirit and all that jazz, my faith in God grew. I never knew Him. God. I never knew Him. I never had the advantage of hearing Bible stories growing up, a praying mother, a father on the deacon board or wearing a white dress while singing in a choir. No. I was the unchurched. Born to parents who were crushing the music entertainment business in Jamaica, I was raised in a predominantly Rastafarian environment. Our dietary restrictions, the fact we grew marijuana in our backyard and took family pictures with blunts in our mouths as a 5 year old would have been odd to others but normal to us.

Greeting the large Ras Tafari portrait on our way out the door or walking up the stairs painted in the red, gold and green indigenous to the faith, not eating pork under any circumstances was a way of life for us. The only thing I knew about God in Heaven was He was mean as an injured dog. He sent the people He created out of the Garden of Eden for real! So hard pass on the Christian God for me.

Yet, here I am in 1992 entrenched in Bible School and insatiably hungry to learn about this same God. At this point there was a little breathing room and I was finally thinking, okay, good things can happen. I had been alive up to this point. I was in my right mind at this point. Not quite sure how both those scenarios happened at the same time. Maybe I was 6 when I began experiencing life as I'd know it. My parents divorced in a very hostile way, meaning they fist fought each other and I witnessed it. I learned later I almost died as an infant when my navel almost bled out; but back to

experiencing life. I was sent with my mom, who I absolutely hated. She spanked and beat me, terrorized me as I saw it. I currently have a split in my eyebrow from my head being hit against the sink. I have scars on my legs from being spanked with a gold metal scaled belt. I wouldn't have known she was on crack and her hostile behavior wasn't because she hated me. It was because she was an addict – a chaotic whirlwind of wild, untamed energy, glorious one moment, diabolical the next.

My father toured the word for music. My mother was absent on her binges. Parentless, in a sense, it's not farfetched to note my first sexual molestation was at 7 on the roof of some apartments next door by an older boy who pinned me down. Guess I was too small to penetrate. Next a group of boys trapped me in the house of my friend. Then, an older girl. Then, an older man, and another of those and another boy and another group of boys. Somehow, I escaped them, not unscathed, but still in tact. I didn't escape the pastor, though, who used manipulation, pills and position to assault…

Between running away from home as a teenager, staying in the ghetto from time to time, stealing food, being in perpetual trouble, seasons without electricity, water or someone to stand up for you – I'd say, I got used to experiencing life.

Life wasn't kind. Yet, I pressed on because something inside of me just refuses to quit.

Then February 28, 1992 happened. I am in class when the Bible school office calls and says the Director wants to see me. What now, I mused. I can't be on any more probations, expulsion is the only option. What in the world have I done now? I walked up the pathway to the office to be led into a room filled with men, who had ghastly expressions and my nerves began fraying. I'm not comfortable like this. The director says, "Sara, I just got a call. I am sorry to tell you that your mother was murdered this morning." No. No. I felt my heart rip to pieces in the same way hers was stabbed to shreds by a knife. I lost my breath. My mind reeled. I wanted to run. I began losing it. How? Why God? What else can I go through? I'm barely able to hold up and now this. Where are you in this? How do I believe? I began collapsing and fighting. The men are now there to restrain me from freaking out. I fell limp. I had nothing left. No sound, no strength, nothing.

But God. Are you there? I search and ask. My heart settles and I know the God that preserved me from all those assaults, who provided for me when I had no food, who sheltered me when I had no lights…. The

God who stood by me when I was counted out, who loved me when I was unlovable, who gave me a purpose when I was problematic … this God, I serve this God and in the middle of this I could feel He was still able to find me, heal me, hold me, console me, build me, propel me. So I breathed and like the woman with the issue of blood, I believed again. I looked back at the milestones and altars. I remembered His goodness, meditated on His kindness and set my faith like Abraham, who against all odds believed Him who promised, for He is faithful. Little by little, day by day, I chose to remember God loves me best even in the worst of circumstances. I didn't know I could handle anymore, but I didn't have to handle it on my own this time around. I could take my tears, my grief, my hurt, my shame, my pain; lift it up on wings of trust and **believe anyway.**

Life isn't always easy and I can't tell you I haven't had other hard things to process.

I have. I will. I decided in spite of it all, the thing that is most important is the thing that has remained – God is faithful and even in this, whatever this is you're dealing with; He is able. Believe Him anyway. He's the come through God! I'm telling you what I know – you can live again.

SARA CONNER

Pastor Sara is the assistant pastor of Word of Truth Family Church, alongside her husband Eben. They have two children, Heaven and London. Sara is a dynamic speaker and author. You can connect with her on Instagram @pastorsara and benefit from many resources you will find at www.pastorsara.com.

OBEY NOW.

UNDERSTAND
LATER.

Believe

TRUST & OBEY NOW, UNDERSTAND LATER

We sounded like a broken record. We said this so many times when our boys were young. We tried to teach them that there would be occasions when we may not have time to explain. If that's the case, it's important to trust us, as parents, and trust in the fact that we have their best interests in mind. We would tell them to obey immediately, and ask questions later, if need be.

We tried to tell our kids "why" when we could. We did not want to leave things at the level of "because we said so!"

We reserved the "because we said so" card for the rare times that they simply needed to obey now and understand later. Our hopes in parenting this principle were that, when they got older, they would have this kind of trust and respect for their teachers and, later, employers.

There is a general lack of respect for authority these days that needs to be restored because there are times at work, in church, and in life that this mindset is needed. I see this thought process being effective in a family setting, especially so, now that the boys are older. The way it plays out now, with us as a family, is that we trust each other and believe the best when there are things we don't understand. Because this has been part of the culture of our family, it's natural to be patient and realize that maybe there is just something we aren't understanding about a situation, rather than going straight to assuming the worst.

Let's look at these examples from scripture of obeying first and understanding later:

"By faith Abraham, when called to go to a place he would later receive as his inheritance, obeyed and went, even though he did not know where he was going." **Hebrews 11:8 NIV**

"But the men who had gone up with him said, "We can't attack those people; they are stronger than we are." 32 And they spread among the Israelites a bad report about the land they had explored. They said, "The land we explored devours those living in it. All the people we saw there are of great size. 33 We saw the Nephilim there (the descendants of Anak come from the Nephilim). We seemed like grasshoppers in our own eyes, and we looked the same to them." **Numbers 13:31-33, NIV**

Logically, it didn't make sense in either of these stories from scripture to simply obey. Has God ever asked you to do something illogical, that didn't make sense to you? When we trust Him anyway, we define the act of having faith. That's what it looks like to "believe ANYWAY."

GET IT? This type of faith is sort of like salvation. If we can actually believe in the whole salvation message of Christ, isn't everything else easy from there? Think for a second on what we believe in. It's wild. It's amazing. It's as far out as anything else God could ever ask us to do. Simply being a Christian, alone, takes faith; nevermind living out all of the other aspects of Christianity.

It takes faith to sit in a chair, faith that the chair won't drop from beneath you. When we sit in a chair, we are indirectly expressing our belief in the person who made that chair. Without saying anything we are expressing faith that these were able workmen, skilled enough to make a chair so that it can hold us up.

We sit in chairs all day long and never even think twice about it. Can we not trust the God who made this entire universe with an understanding that says, when we fall into His loving arms, He will catch us?

Yes! An emphatic Yes! We can! It's just that, sometimes, it requires us to trust and obey, then understand later.

"Trust in the Lord with all your heart and lean not on your own understanding."

Proverbs 3:5 (NKJV)

Believer

Think of three people you feel drawn to, a job you feel drawn to or a big step of obedience you know God is leading you into. Ask God to reveal to you one act of obedience that may or may not make sense, but you know it is something that will lead to a good result if you are faithful to obey first and understand later. What is He leading you to do?

_____

_____

Sometimes we have to believe in our hearts, even when our heads are fighting us the whole way. Brother Kenneth E. Hagin often said that we can believe in our hearts, while having doubt in our heads. When I first heard him say these things, it gave me so much relief.

Let's get real. We are not super-human and there are times when we have to "do it afraid," just like Joyce Meyer says. I went to her conference the same year that was the theme. Do it Afraid. Goodness. That concept so perfectly complements this chapter because it is exactly what we have to do when we decide to obey God even though we don't understand.

> "The fear of the Lord is the beginning of wisdom." **Prov. 9:10 NIV**

When we fear (respect, trust) God over whatever or whoever we are facing, wisdom and understanding come to us. The more we renew our minds with the Word, while constantly seeking His wisdom, the more we will think like

God does and the more we will actually understand.

Eventually, as our minds are transformed by the Word of God, we will begin to more readily walk in obedience with or without having to understand everything. Yielding to God's will becomes more and more second nature. We live out a holy, consecrated life that looks like this statement spoken by Jesus: "Not my will, Lord, but yours be done! If this cup can pass from me, please let it, but if not, let's do this!" Luke 22:42 (Paraphrased)

Also, He shows us things to come when He deems it needful. Yet, during the times He doesn't reveal upcoming events, that is when we believe Him ANYWAY, no matter how it looks, or how much we don't understand.

This process describes what it looks like to be willing and obedient. It reveals how this obedience will cause us to "…eat the good of the land!"

John 16:13, Isaiah 1:19

Abraham didn't understand but went to the altar to sacrifice Isaac in obedience and found God to be faithful. There was a ram in the thicket!

If you are in a jam and need a "ram in the thicket," just keep obeying and believing ANYWAY that God will provide. Then, just like it happened with Abraham, you will learn that God is no respecter of people and He will deliver you in the nick of time.

Really think about this story for a minute. Think about the humility it took for

Abraham to trust God in this manner. It makes me think of James 4:7 that says to submit to God, resist the devil and he will flee.

I LOVE THE WAY ED YOUNG SAYS, "GET UNDER WHAT YOU NEED TO GET UNDER, SO YOU CAN GET OVER WHAT YOU NEED TO GET OVER!"

Do you need to humble yourself to someone in your life and get under their authority, so that you can get over some stuff going on in your life that is directly connected to your lack of honor towards someone?

Ask God to help you get under "who" or "what" you need to get under, so you can get over what you need to get over and write down what He speaks to you:

_____

_____

Learning to obey first and understanding later is among the most important keys to success in life. This type of teachability can get you promoted at work faster than anything. Mastering this concept can keep your child safe when you say to them in a parking lot, "STOP!" They will be rescued from the car coming, whose driver may not see them due to their three-foot stature.

This is how it is with us and God. We have the toddler's perspective of the world compared to His expansive perspective. If we can really get this deep down into the fabric of our beings, maybe then we could truly trust Him and be doers of these scriptures…

> "Now faith is the substance of things hoped for, the evidence of things not seen." **Hebrews 11:1 KJV**
>
> "We walk by faith, not by sight." **2 Corinthians 5:7 NJKV**

It's been said that faith and patience are the power twins. It's hard to believe now and receive later. I can be like a three-year-old running into the parking lot, headed for the ice cream store - because I want it NOW! Have you been there too?

To a child, when Mom says no, and holds the child back from the ice cream parlor for only a minute or two until the car goes by, it seems like an eternity. That crying child, who fears her fun is being spoiled, thinks her wait is an eternal one. Yet the mom knows it will only hold off the fun for a few moments. In the process, she saved the child's life.

People possess differing perspectives. The clueless toddler may never know, regarding that particular outing, about mom's lifesaving effort. In her youth, she may not be capable of understanding why it was so important not to run toward what she wanted in that very moment.

Real faith rests.

Think about the story of the toddler wanting the ice cream.

Had she trusted that her mother knew best, and that she would get her ice cream soon enough, she would not have thrown a fit. Instead, she would have rested in her mom's embrace. Can we relate to this in more adult scenarios?

> "For we which have believed do enter into rest…" **Hebrews 4:3 KJV**

What are you going through right now that has caused you to need to rest in God's embrace and trust the process, even though you don't understand?

The Science of Believing:

Simon Sinek produced the third most popular TED video of all time.

Sinek, who is the author of Start with Why, Leaders Eat Last, and Together is Better started a movement in 2009 by helping employers inspire their employees by starting with "Why?" instead of "How? What? or When?

The thought is that people won't buy a product, service or into a movement or a company unless they understand the "Why?" and are inspired by it. Furthermore, what has been found through studies is that "How?" can stifle action, growth, and creativity. Come back to the "How?" after you are first, and most importantly, engaged with "Why?" Next is the "What?"

Have you ever heard "Where there is a will there is a way"? Maybe you've heard "figure it out along the way", or, "just do it"? I think these cliché's have come from people who decided to just "go for it," even if they didn't have it all figured it out. Another cliché that comes to mind is that it's easier to steer a moving car than a parked one.

Of course, planning is important, but overthinking the "how" and "what if's" can lead to paralysis by analysis which kills productivity. It makes me think of the title of this chapter…Obey Now, Understand Later. This is the same concept! Get going in the direction you know you are supposed to go, and understanding will come as you walk toward your Divine destiny.

Overthinking can lower your performance on mentally demanding tasks as much as can high stress situations and high-pressure jobs.

Overthinking kills creativity.

Grace Hawthorne, a professor at The Stanford University Institute of Design, partnered with behavioral scientist Allan Reiss to find a way to scientifically measure creativity by using brain imaging:

"Participants in the study were placed into a functional magnetic resonance imaging machine with a nonmagnetic tablet and asked to draw a series of pictures based on action words (for example, vote, exhaust, salute) with thirty seconds for each word. They also drew a zigzag line to establish baseline brain function for the task of drawing. The participants later ranked each word picture based on its difficulty to draw. The tablet transmitted the drawings to researchers who scored them on a 5-point scale of creativity, and researchers at the School of Medicine who analyzed the MRI scans for brain activity patterns.

The results were surprising: the prefrontal cortex, traditionally associated with thinking, was most active for the drawings the participants ranked as most difficult; the cerebellum [the part of the brain traditionally associated with movement] was most active for the drawings the participants scored highest on for creativity. Essentially, the less the participants thought about what they were drawing, the more creative their drawings were.

This study suggests that overthinking a problem makes it more difficult to do your very best creative work.

https://www.scientificamerican.com/article/don-t-overthink-it-less-is-more-when-it-comes-to-creativity/

Overthinking eats up your willpower.

The National Academy of Science reported a fascinating study.

It was also something most scholars also found to be quite alarming. They studied the rulings of parole board judges over 10 months.

They found judges were significantly more likely to grant parole earlier in the morning and immediately after a food break. Cases presented before judges at the end of long sessions were far more likely to be denied. This phenomenon held true over a whopping 1,100 cases no matter the severity of each crime.

What this means for you and me is that the more time we spend within our workdays focusing on the how, when, where, and what, the more fatigued we will be and the more likely our decisions will be skewed in a manner that causes a decrease in our productivity. When we start with the why and are sold on it, that helps automatically answer many questions and details with much less effort. Anytime we can automate things, the simpler they are right?

People like Martin Luther King Jr., Steve Jobs, and the Wright Brothers had little in common, except they all started with WHY!

Let's take a hint from this science of believing and start with the "Why." God has said that we should trust and obey what He is leading us into. He requires us to trust Him for the understanding, as we need to know.

https://www.pnas.org/content/pnas/108/17/6889.full.pdf

Don't Stop Believing!

Spiritual	Personal	Family	Social	Financial	Career	Health

For this chapter, let's look at the Social basket of life.

Obeying the phrase, "to have a friend, be a friend," has resulted in the creation of some of my closest friendships. Proverbs 18:24

At one point in my life, I cried out to God, "I need a friend!"

I would tell Him how I was a good friend to other individuals. I would call out names of the dear friends I had in high school, and though I wasn't a perfect friend, I was a good friend to many.

In those moments, I was at the throne of God, making my requests known to Him, like the Word teaches us to do. I was ready to reap what I had faithfully sown into other friendships.

Today, I am absolutely overwhelmed and blown away with all the meaningful friendships I am blessed with. Some of the most amazing people I know actually call me their friend. I find myself both honored and humbled. When we invest in relationships, what we reap is really what life is all about; a love from out of this world and the fulfillment of all we are all looking for.

Let's discuss your social goals.

Who are some of your friends that you are most thankful for?

_____

_____

MY SOCIAL GOALS

At the end of my life, I will be fulfilled in the social aspect of my life if _____.

In five years, when I look back to this day _____ _____ will have happened for me to be able to say, "Yes! My social life is just how I want it to be."

In one year, I will be able to describe the relationships that mean the most to me like this:

_____

_____

In three months, these social goals must be accomplished in order to be on track for my one year, five year, and lifetime goals to become a reality:

_____

_____

(Examples: go to coffee with a friend weekly, go on a double date monthly, or think of three people you are patiently praying for your relationship to become healthier with. Write down three things you can do to invest into a particular relationship and give yourself a deadline for each over the next three months.)

This week I will make 3-5 tasks a priority because they are in line with what I believe God is showing me is His plan for my social life. I will rise early and be diligent this week to get these things done in order to reach my goals:

_____

_____

(Example: send an encouraging note in the mail to your closest friends, break up with that guy who is toxic for you, set boundaries within a relationship, or call your friend who lives far away and catch up.)

When I get discouraged, I will think of all that I have to be thankful for, when it comes to my friends and colleagues. These are a few things I am most thankful for.

_____

_____

you sooooooo got this, girl!

This is what we will call the H.O.P.E. process. It's the part of Believe ANYWAY where you will dig deeper into the scripture and mine out jewels that I believe God intends to speak to you in profound ways. Find the verses from this chapter that stand out most to you and put these verses through the **H.O.P.E. process.** The "H" stands for **His story.** Simply write out a verse from this chapter. The "O" stands for **Observation**. Ask God to show you what He wants you to observe from this verse the most. Write down what He speaks to you. The "P" stands for **Prayer.** Write out your prayer regarding this verse. What are you needing or wanting to see in your life? Ask Him for it. The "E" is for **Expectation** and this is where you will write out by faith, in present or past tense, what you expect to become reality in your life. Faith is now the substance of things hoped for and the evidence of things not yet seen as Hebrews tells us. This is where our hope turns into faith and brings things from the future into our present.

H IS STORY

_____

_____

O BSERVATION

_____

_____

P RAYER

_____

_____

E XPECTATION

_____

_____

H IS STORY

_____

_____

_____

O BSERVATION

_____

_____

_____

P RAYER

_____

_____

_____

E XPECTATION

_____

_____

_____

H IS STORY

_____

_____

_____

O BSERVATION

_____

_____

_____

P RAYER

_____

_____

_____

E XPECTATION

_____

_____

_____

H IS STORY

_____

_____

_____

O BSERVATION

_____

_____

_____

P RAYER

_____

_____

_____

E XPECTATION

_____

_____

_____

H IS STORY

_____

_____

_____

O BSERVATION

_____

_____

_____

P RAYER

_____

_____

_____

E XPECTATION

_____

_____

_____

Complete this maze by starting with "Obey"
and ending on "Understand"

START: "Obey"

"Understand" END:

I Chose to Believe Anyway...

and this is what happened...

"Pittsburgh", one word that would change my life forever! I was 23 years old when I very clearly heard that one word from the Lord.

God had so graciously asked my husband and I to move across the country and pioneer a church in Pittsburgh, Pennsylvania. Up to this point my travel experience was minimal, other than vacations with the family and driving to Dallas for a shopping weekend;). I had no idea the days, months, years and decades of building God's House that lie ahead. I didn't care! I was fired up! I was full of faith! I was ready to change the world! It was easy to believe that God was with us, He had called us, He was equipping us, He was changing lives and He was moving in Steeler Country!

Bible School had left us ready to preach & ready to reach the world for Christ. It was like living the dream (I call it the honeymoon stage:). We would believe God for chairs & they would show up. We would believe God for a sound system and one would show up. We would believe God for musicians and they would show up. We would believe God for finances and the money would show up. It was all good until... we kept running into a specific 'believe God for' problem, over and over again. We would move into a building, work on an arrangement to purchase the building, the deal would fall through and we would have to find a new building. This happened at least 7 times in 15 years and we really needed our own building! We were a young church and moving your location 7 times was not the best strategy. Our faith to own a church building was shaken.

One particular building transaction, the owner stole $300,000 from our church that was going toward the purchase. It was frustrating, disappointing, and heartbreaking to say the least. We just couldn't gain ground in this area.

I might be a grownup pastor but the first person I would call and tell about our problems were my parents! Every single time I would tell my mom about this horrible building situation she would say, "I believe God is going to give you a free building." Ok, whatever mom. The next bummer building situation I would call mom, she would say "I believe someone is going to give you a free building." I listened

to her and it was getting into my heart but we had just moved into a movie theater for church services. Seriously God?! Is it time to bounce out of here? We needed stability. We made a decision to stay at the movie theater and 'believe God for' His timing with a building.

Several years passed, the church was growing and we went on the building hunt again. The first call we made, "Hello, we are interested in purchasing this piece of property." "What exactly are you looking to do?," they replied. "We are building a church," we said on the line.

Their reply is one that is forever tattooed on my heart, "Would you be interested in a furniture building with 5 acres on a busy highway for a tax write off?"

God gave us a free building, with 5 acres on the busiest road east of Pittsburgh! God was waiting all those years to set us up for a free building in the best location! Since then, we've added 60 acres to that, with a daycare and several other businesses! Add to that another new campus location on the busiest road in the north of Pittsburgh! We have the best church locations, the best buildings, in His perfect timing!

I know you're disappointed & frustrated.

I know it doesn't always look like God is working.

Stay teachable, be humble and keep your hopes up! When it looks like it's not going to work out - Believe Anyway.

You can ALWAYS trust God! He has something better for you and His timing is ALWAYS perfect!

AMY SCHAFER

Amy Schafer is the Co-Lead Pastor of Grace Life Church with locations in the east & north of Pittsburgh, Pennsylvania. Grace Life Church is a thriving, multi-cultural, multi-generational church that has become a model & leading voice for unity in PGH since 1997. Amy also works with Cornerstone Televison Network as a co-host on two of their programs --"Hope Today" and "Sister-to-Sister".

Amy loves to see people planted in God's House and flourishing in life. She is also known for her bold faith, fun spirit, strong leadership and creative ideas.

Married for 25 years, she is also a wife and busy parent of three awesome children—Gloria-21, Gabe-16, and Judah-13

WEEK SIX

I

STILL

BELIEVE

Believe

YOUR PROMISES ARE TRUE

"Abraham staggered not at the promise through unbelief but was strong in faith, giving glory to God and was fully persuaded that He would come through on His promises." Romans 4:20-21 (Paraphrased)

Are you strong in faith, right now, concerning what you are going through, fully persuaded that He will come through for you? Or are you staggering at the promise through unbelief? What trips you up most often?

_____

_____

"My thoughts are nothing like your thoughts," says the LORD. "And my ways are far beyond anything you could imagine." Isaiah 55:8, NLT

What are your real, honest thoughts on your current, most difficult, situation right now?

_____

_____

Ask yourself if these thoughts line up with what God says in His Word? Have you asked God to show You His thoughts on the matter?

"Make sure that your character is free from the love of money, being content with what you have; for He Himself has said, 'I WILL NEVER DESERT YOU, NOR WILL I EVER FORSAKE YOU'," Hebrews 13:5 NASB

So often, whether we have lost a job, are going through financial struggles - big or small - hustling like crazy trying to keep up with the Jones family, even with divorce, an affair, or loss of a loved one, having enough money becomes a big part of the fear that can paralyze us. Maybe I shouldn't admit this to you, but after graduating from three Bible schools, I somehow never realized these two statements were connected in the same verse! I have now received new understanding of this scripture. I hope this rocks your world as resoundingly as it has mine.

Women, our greatest need is security. When we feel like God has forsaken us or deserted us, we have to understand that He hasn't. He won't. The next time a panic attack tries to set in, or low-grade anxiety creeps in, go to this verse and choose to believe it in the face of whatever is happening. Sit down, look to Jesus, the Author and FINISHER of our faith. Simply decide to trust Him. I know. It feels irresponsible and our natural disposition of being control freaks makes us think we have to worry. News Flash: It's more responsible for us to let go and let God. I've always hated that cliché, thinking it was a copout for lazy people. In all actuality, it is an act of real faith. It is what we do when we go free from the worry of money or any other thing that rocks our security. Letting go, and letting God handle our situations, doesn't excuse us from doing our part. Of course not. But in some of the most devastating pickles we may find ourselves in, guess what? We don't have what it takes to get out of them. It will be only His grace and His ability that will keep us and help us get to the other side.

> "There are some things that the LORD our God has kept secret; but he has revealed his Law, and we and our descendants are to obey it forever." Deuteronomy 29:29 HCSB

Here's the big question. Can you authentically say these statements?

I STILL BELIEVE

→ EVEN WHEN THE DREAM HASN'T COME TO PASS YET.

→ EVEN IF SHE DIED.

→ EVEN WHEN I'VE SCREWED UP THINGS.

I STILL BELIEVE IN YOUR PLAN FOR MY LIFE AND FOR MY FAMILY

If not, let's talk....maybe this will be what could really help you to be able to still believe on the drabbest of days. It is something that helps me so much. When I don't understand and I can't make 2+2=4 in my life, this verse is so comforting to me. And guess what? While studying Deuteronomy 29:29, I realized something. Though there are times when we just have to sort of throw our hands up in the air and say, "Well, the secret thing belongs to the Lord, and I may not understand, but I choose to trust that God either knows something I don't know (Ya think!) or maybe something has happened that there is no seemingly good reason for and seems so horrible. It is in these moments that we have to make a choice to be a believer or an unbeliever. Notice that the second part of the verse could be the answer to keep us steady in uncertain times, times when we don't understand. What I'm saying is that His law and His principles are there for us to obey (and live by forever) no matter what. This is huge. If we would just be people of principle, following what He has revealed to us in His Word, then when the boat is rocking, and the seas are roaring, we can stay steady as long as we forever follow His ways, even when there are things we don't understand. This is such a key to being able to honestly say, "I still believe...ANYWAY."

HIS WORD OVER THEIR WORDS

When we are totally convinced that the Bible is true and it is the infallible Word of God, then we can bank on what God says. We can know that it is more powerful in our lives than what anyone else says. When we hear bad news or get a bad report from the doctor, it is time to cling to His every Word. This is where we find the peace and joy to get us through.

The more our hearts are filled with His Word, the more we speak what He says rather than what we hear others say. Scripture tells us, out of the abundance of the heart our mouths speak. Have you ever noticed that friends who speak more of what God says, rather than repeating gossip or negative news, are more fun to be around? When we speak His Word, we speak life. People are attracted to life-giving words, over doom and gloom, any day! But what if we are surrounded by doom and gloom? That's when we can choose to sing the lyrics of the song that says, "It may look like I'm surrounded, but I'm surrounded by You!" by Michael W. Smith.

Think of it. God formed this entire world with Words. We are made in His image. We form our worlds with our words! When our mouths bless those around us with the Word of God, it literally gives life to people and causes things to revive that were dying. Sadly, the opposite of this is also true.

> Proverbs 6:2 NKJV "You are snared by the words of your mouth."

Today, let's consecrate our mouths to say what God says about our lives. As we do this, we will thrive no matter what is thrown at us.

> "And we know that all things work together for good to those who love God, to those who are the called according to His purpose." Romans 8:28 NKJV

We experience this verse in our lives as we become more and more convinced of His promises. They are "Yes" and "Amen," as scripture says. Let's say what He says. Let's ignore what others say. Let's not be our own worst critic either, instead speaking life over our lives and all of those around us. Let's ask God to take the coal and cleanse our lips, Lord! Here we are! Isaiah 6:7

"And we know that all things work together for good to those who love God, to those who are called according to His purpose."

Romans 8:28 (NKJV)

God is so great at working things out for our good that all too often He gets blamed for causing the suffering we go through to teach us something. Let's think about this theology for a second. When your child was small and you told him not to touch the hot stove, what did he do? Touched it anyway! Did you commission him to touch the hot stove? No loving parent would do that. Did you permit or allow it? You probably just couldn't keep him from it, could you? He chose to do it while you weren't looking. You then probably consoled him and cared for him, as any loving parent would.

Yes, God is sovereign. Yes! He has given us a free will. It really goes all the way back to the garden, when God gave mankind dominion in the earth. Sin entered the world due to man refusing to obey then and understand later. Consequently, the devil became the god of this world and mankind no longer had dominion. Jesus came and bought our authority back. We now have it again in/through Christ. So, with this delegated authority from God, we have a choice to receive all that Jesus came to procure for us - or not. When we resist the devil and submit to God, the devil has to flee because this is what Jesus came back to restore. Abundant life. He bore our sin, sickness, poverty, and the frustration of our peace on the Cross.

(Isaiah 53:4-5, II Corinthians 8:9)

It is up to us. We can walk in the spiritual, physical, and mental salvation Jesus legally bought back for us. It is there for the taking. His grace is sufficient. It is finished. The fight is fixed. Let's obey now, understand later. These are the keys to walking in all that is ours through the atonement. It may not look the way we had imagined exactly, but even when it doesn't, God is the Potter and we are the clay. No doubt, He will make something beautiful of our messes!

The Science of Believing:

Many science experiments don't turn out exactly the way those conducting them thought they would. In fact, in certain instances, medicine can be created for one thing, but then it is discovered that it actually treats something else even more effectively than what it was originally designed for. So maybe, along the way, they may have thought something was a failure, but in reality, it just turned out to be successful differently.

I remember doing science projects with my kids when they were in elementary and middle school. They would write down their hypothesis and then test whichever project it was at the time, whether a catapult or a volcano. One time it was all about measuring the distance and speed of a rolling soccer ball; not sure I remember the exact point of that one. Gosh! Those were the days. Confession: I loved school projects. All of my friends would complain about them. But to me, they were built-in times my boys had to spend time with me because they needed my help. Before you judge me, they did their own projects, but I was right there soaking up every memory and moment I could with them. Anyway, point being, many of their projects ended up with a different result than the hypotheses, but the cool thing about it was, as long as you properly notated the study, the result really didn't matter and didn't affect the grade. It all was more about the process than the result.

Much the same, things may not go like we had hoped. Circumstances may leave us with a huge question mark. That's when we can choose to believe even though things don't always turn out the way we thought they would; God is a God that He should not lie. His faithfulness is forever. His perspective is flawless. His ways are higher than ours and His love for us never fails. Life simply stinks sometimes, but He can make a way when there seems to be no way, even if it is a different way from how we started.

Don't Stop Believing!

| Spiritual | Personal | Family | Social | Financial | Career | Health |

For this chapter, let's look at the basket of your finances and see what your goals are. This is certainly a part of life that we have to STILL believe in often, isn't it? I believe this exercise is going to set your finances on a course that will help you thrive like never before. If you will stick to it! Let God lengthen your chords and expand your vision in this part of your life. God wants to bless you to be a blessing. As you do this activity, try to think about money from a place of abundance and not lack. God is a God of more than enough. He is just looking for ways to bless you, give you witty ideas, guide you, and lead you.

> "O fear the Lord, ye His saints; for there is no want to them that fear Him." Psalm 34:9 KJV

His Word also says, in Deuteronomy 28:8, that everything you put your hand to prospers, so be in agreement with His Word as you complete this exercise. If you need to boost your faith a little more in this area, look up these verses and choose to believe ANYWAY regarding your finances.

Deuteronomy 28:2 // Isaiah 1:19
1 Timothy 6:17-18 // Philippians 4:19 // 3 John 2

MY FINANCIAL GOALS

At the end of my life, I will have succeeded financially if

_____

_____

In five years, when I look back to this day _____
_____will have
happened for me to be able to say, "Yes! I did it!"

(amount of annual income, amount saved, house purchased, Given 10+% to my church and missions, etc, fun had)

In one year, I will make $ ___ /yr, save $___ /yr, give___ $/ yr, and enjoy $___ /yr.

In three months, these goals must be done in order to be on track for my one year, five year, and lifetime goals to become a reality:

_____

_____

This week, I will make 3-5 tasks a priority because they are in line with what I believe God is showing me is His plan for my life financially. I will rise early and be diligent this week to get these things done in order to reach my goals:

_____

_____

When I get discouraged, I will think of all that I have to be thankful for when it comes to my finances. These are a few things I am most thankful for:

_____

_____

Okay, now ask God to show you what you can do to get better in these areas and for the resources to be able to do what He is calling you to do. Ask Him if He would like to speak to you regarding direction in this area of your life. Or if you need correction? Or just anything else? What is He saying?

Girl Be Brave!

Cheryl Hale

This is what we will call the H.O.P.E. process. It's the part of Believe ANYWAY where you will dig deeper into the scripture and mine out jewels that I believe God intends to speak to you in profound ways. Find the verses from this chapter that stand out most to you and put these verses through the **H.O.P.E. process.** The "H" stands for **His story.** Simply write out a verse from this chapter. The "O" stands for **Observation**. Ask God to show you what He wants you to observe from this verse the most. Write down what He speaks to you. The "P" stands for **Prayer.** Write out your prayer regarding this verse. What are you needing or wanting to see in your life? Ask Him for it. The "E" is for **Expectation** and this is where you will write out by faith, in present or past tense, what you expect to become reality in your life. Faith is now the substance of things hoped for and the evidence of things not yet seen as Hebrews tells us. This is where our hope turns into faith and brings things from the future into our present.

H IS STORY _____

O BSERVATION _____

P RAYER _____

E XPECTATION _____

H IS STORY

_____

_____

_____

O BSERVATION

_____

_____

_____

P RAYER

_____

_____

_____

E XPECTATION

_____

_____

_____

H IS STORY

_____

_____

_____

O BSERVATION

_____

_____

_____

P RAYER

_____

_____

_____

E XPECTATION

_____

_____

_____

H IS STORY

_____

_____

_____

O BSERVATION

_____

_____

_____

P RAYER

_____

_____

_____

E XPECTATION

_____

_____

_____

H IS STORY

_____

_____

_____

_____

O BSERVATION

_____

_____

_____

P RAYER

_____

_____

_____

E XPECTATION

_____

_____

_____

PRAY. DREAM. GOAL. REPEAT

Write your prayers, dreams, and goals in steps to lead you to your end goal. Start at the end and work backwards. Take a picture of this and make it your screen saver so you see it all the time. As things take shape, be ok that they may not turn out exactly how you wished for them to, but believe God that your steps are ordered of the Lord and that His ways are even higher than yours.

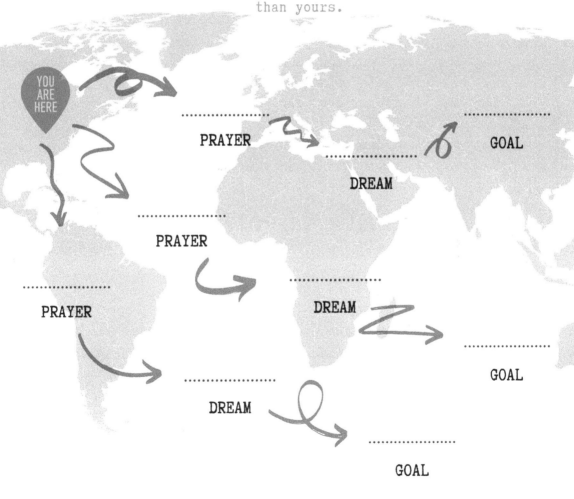

YOU ARE HERE

PRAYER

PRAYER

PRAYER

DREAM

DREAM

DREAM

GOAL

GOAL

GOAL

I Chose to Believe Anyway...

and this is what happened...

I've been married twice. I thought my first husband was the man of my dreams! We had a fairy-tale wedding… he even cried as I walked down the aisle! Our marriage was so AWESOME… for three whole weeks!

One Wednesday night, he didn't come home from work, I was sure that he was stopping to get me flowers (After all, it was my birthday week). By 1:00 am, I'd called his mother, all the hospitals, and the police. Saturday morning turned into Saturday night. Why didn't he call? I finally fell asleep, exhausted from crying all day. Sunday morning turned into Sunday night (still no word) and I started to think that I'd never see him again.

That's when he BURST through the door in a fit of anger! He'd gotten paid on Friday and blown his entire paycheck on crack cocaine! When he ran out of money, that's when he came home to hurt me. In and out of rehab, I still thought we could somehow work through this. Love will keep us together, right?

He maxed out all our credit cards. He sold all the furniture out of our house (stuff we were still making payments on). He stole my son's Nintendo and pawned it for drug money. He got so violent that he broke my rib and herniated a disk in my neck when he threw me through a wall! Even restraining orders didn't slow him down.

(Just give me a screwdriver. Even to this day, I can change out a deadbolt lock in under five minutes!)

160

I don't know how many times I prayed, "God, SAVE my marriage! God, make him love ME more than he loves drugs!" It was the most painful time of my life! I couldn't figure it out. I thought, for sure, God had FAILED ME. But God says, "Trust Me! My ways are not your ways. I'm so much bigger than you can ask, think, or imagine!" **Believe ANYWAY!**

Now when I look at my life, my husband, David, my family, my calling, and my ministry; when I look at the special insight and revelation I now have to speak to hurting people…. I realize that God didn't fail me at all. I believed and I came THROUGH! God never wavered. He was ALWAYS there, protecting and preparing me for this ministry. I'm exactly where I'm supposed to be!

Believe ANYWAY – Even When You Think God Failed!

NICOLE CRANK

Nicole Crank is a dynamic international conference speaker, popular television host, successful pastor, life coach, blogger, and author of a new book, I Will Thrive; where Nicole shares her journey from abandonment, molestation, rape and abuse, to victory! Not just surviving… but with God's help, learning to THRIVE! And you can, too! Her other books include, Goal Getters and two titles in the popular, Hi God Series.

The Nicole Crank Show can be seen around the world on Christian Television Networks and YouTube. Nicole and husband, David, are co-founders and senior pastors of FaithChurch.com, with a membership of over 18,000 at four campuses in St. Louis and two in West Palm Beach, plus thousands more who worship Online! Connect with Nicole, read her weekly blog, sign up for her T12 Transformation Curriculum, and join her Circle of Friends @NicoleCrank.com

HAPPY PEOPLE

TRUST IN

THE LORD

WEEK SEVEN

Believer

> "Happy are those who trust in the Lord."
> Psalm 40:4 (GNB)

Have you ever noticed that the last time you were unhappy, stressed, or worried about something, if you are honest, in that moment, you were not exactly trusting the Lord. In that situation, your weren't standing on His promises, believing that He would, for sure, bring you through. When we worry, we are imagining worst case scenarios, yielding to fear instead of faith, and leaning on our own ability to make things happen.

Are you a let-life-happen person or a make-life-happen person? I am for sure the latter by nature, and if you are too, then you know how hard it is to rest in God. Real faith rests.

Think about it…when are you happiest? On vacation or at work? Snuggled up with the love of your life, even if just in your imagination, while watching a chic flic? Or shuffling papers behind a desk at work with deadlines bearing down on you that are impossible to meet? Umm, bet I can guess which one. I like a challenge and love what I do for a living, but nothing beats being in snuggly jammies, or on the beach, or coffee with a friend without a worry in sight for miles. Are you in sync with me? What if we could have these levels of peace that I just described in our day-to-day lives? Call me crazy. I think we can! Have I figured out how yet? I think so. The short version is this: God is Love is Happy. Have I mastered the skills of this level of happy? Think again. But I am on my way and not stopping until I get there. It's a process for us all, a process of learning how to love ANYWAY, believe ANYWAY, and finally be happy ANYWAY. When we trust God, which takes faith, it affects our ability to be happy ANYWAY. But also, being convinced of God's love for us takes an additional leap of faith to trust Him even when it may not look like it to us. Can you see how this all works together, and how we can't really have one without the other?

What is something you need to decide once and for all to trust the Lord about??

_____

_____

Now, can you believe it's that simple? If you seriously just gave that to Him, then you must feel like a thousand pounds have lifted. You can literally go free from it right now - in a split second! Now don't take it back on. His shoulders are broad enough. Trust Him not to drop it and watch your happiness soar. Describe the difference in your emotional state, as a result of trusting God with this right now.

_____

_____

I encourage you to come back to this section next week and fill in the blanks below as to how you felt and how things have changed for your mental and spiritual health, maybe even physical health, now that you are trusting Him, like never before, for a whole week.

Thoughts to ponder over the next few days, as you go about your daily grind, are whether you are up against dreaded things, like cancer? Or the death of a loved one? Or even just low-grade panic, otherwise known as anxiety? A real key in finding hope in our lives is remaining truly connected to our mindset.

So many of us, maybe even due to past traumatic incidents, live in a state of anxiety. Stress is supposed to be reserved for real emergencies and trauma and then subside, once that incident is over, so our bodies can recoup for when that much adrenaline is needed again. Make sense? God didn't design our bodies to live in a state of worry all the time. He designed us to trust Him. When we do, we are happy. You and I were made to be happy!

Here's a tip from each chapter of my book, Happy ANYWAY. These nuggets of truth will help you trust in the Lord, and as a result, be happy and thrive no matter what life throws at you.

1 - Don't Worry. Be Happy.

Picture yourself throwing the whole of your anxiety and cares onto Jesus. If you have to literally visualize doing this each time you change clothes, do it. Take off anxiety and worry each day and put on peace and joy and love.

1 Peter 5:7 // Ephesians 4:22-24

Journal your thoughts:

_____

_____

_____

_____

2 - Happy Perspective

The Word of God is the clear lens we can look through to really be able to see what is actually going on and how to handle it. When we begin to fear God, more than others or our situations, it changes our perspective to see things the way God sees them, rather than how we naturally see them.

Prov. 9:10 // John 16:13 // 1 Cor. 13:12

Journal your thoughts:

_____

_____

_____

_____

3 - Happy and Healthy

We will prosper and be in health as our soul prospers, so having our mind-set renewed by His Word transforms us. A merry heart does good like a medicine. Also, the degree we guard our hearts will be the degree life flows out of it rather than death. Want to be happy and healthy? I believe this chapter could literally improve your health like it has mine.

3 John // 2 Proverbs 17:22 // Proverbs 4:20

Journal your thoughts:

_____

_____

_____

_____

4 - Happy to help

Deep down, we all want to contribute and serve humanity in some way. God put that in us and we need to achieve His purposes. We need serve fiercely and be as others minded as we are also self-care minded. We will only love others to the degree that we love ourselves well. And we will only love ourselves to the degree we love God and learn how to receive His love. Along these lines, we sometimes need to get better at asking for help, creating boundaries, and being sure we are happy to help and not helping begrudgingly.

Joshua 10:4 // Matt. 22:37-39

Journal your thoughts:

_____

_____

_____

_____

5a - Happy Wife, Happy Life

It's time we take responsibility for the only part of the culture of our homes, offices and atmospheres that we can really do anything about. The part we create. When we walk into a room, we carry an atmosphere with us. What atmosphere are you bringing into the room? A happy one? A stressed one? A critical one? A sad one? It's your choice. Your relationships will change to a great degree when you sow life, instead of nagging and complaining.

Prov. 27:15 // Ephesians 5:22-23

Journal your thoughts:

_____

_____

_____

_____

5ab – Happy and Available

If you are single, don't go looking for a guy. It is his job to find you. Concentrate on being the treasure he is looking for. And focus on creating a mindset that is becoming of you. Your prince charming will notice, no doubt!

Colossians 2:10 // Colossians 3:1-4

Journal your thoughts:

_____

_____

_____

6 – Happy Habits

Hope yourself happy

by anchoring your hope in Christ. **Hebrews 6:19**

One way is to have a growth mindset, rather than a fixed mindset. A growth mindset is one of hope, while a fixed mindset says this is just how it is.

Get off the Not-So-Merry-Go-Round.

No more if/then happiness. If I could only be or have….. then I would be happy. No more comparing up. Learn how to increase your happiness set point.

Find your strengths. Find your happy.

Learn what your strengths are and live from them, instead of focusing on what you need to improve all the time.

Talk Happy. Walk Happy.

We frame our world by the words that come out of our mouths. Speak life to others. Change your self-talk. Watch things change all around you.

Create and enjoy happy emotions.

Optimists live longer. It's been scientifically proven, so learn how to become more of a positive person and improve your life - and quite possibly the longevity of it.

Own your happy.

Decide right now that no one gets to choose whether or not they can ruin your day or take away your joy.

Spread the happy.

When you make others happy, it's the completion of the law of sowing and reaping. Nothing else makes us happier.

Plan your happy.

Get a vision. Write it down. Keep it in front of your eyes and encourage yourself with it often.

This chapter is a tiny little taste of Happy ANYWAY. If you enjoyed this chapter, you have GOTTA get Happy ANYWAY so that you can really dig into more of how to happy. I hope to join you in Happy ANYWAY as you continue on this journey with me to thrive like you were made to do!

Which Happy Habits are you pretty good at and which ones do you need to develop more in your life?

_____

_____

_____

_____

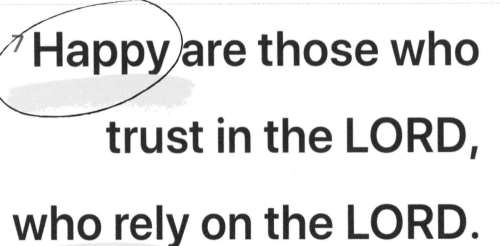

⁷ Happy are those who

trust in the LORD,

who rely on the LORD.

The Science of Believing:

HAPPY PEOPLE LIVE LONGER.

You read that right. Optimists live longer than pessimists! Did you know that?

Check out this research: Having an optimistic mind-set may reduce the risk for cardiovascular disease and early death.

In previous studies, optimism has been shown to be associated with a range of favorable, physical health outcomes and with greater success in work, school and relationships.

This new meta-analysis, published in JAMA Network Open, included fifteen studies that measured optimism and pessimism by asking the level of agreement with such statements as "In uncertain times, I usually expect the best," or "I rarely expect good things to happen to me."

Analysis of the ten studies that looked at heart disease, which pooled data on 209,436 people, found that compared with pessimists, people with the most optimistic outlook had a 35% lower risk for cardiovascular events.

Nine studies with data on all-cause mortality included 188,599 participants and found that optimists had a 14% lower risk of premature death than the most pessimistic people.

The studies had an average fourteen-year follow-up for various health and behavioral characteristics, including a wide range of cardiovascular disease risk factors.

"It seems optimists have better health behaviors," said the lead author, Dr. Alan Rozanski, a professor of medicine at the Icahn School of Medicine at Mount Sinai. "They're more likely to exercise and to have better diet. And there is evidence of direct biological effects — they have less inflammation and fewer metabolic abnormalities."

https://www.nytimes.com/2019/09/27/well/mind/a-positive-outlook-may-be-good-for-your-heart.html

Don't Stop Believing!

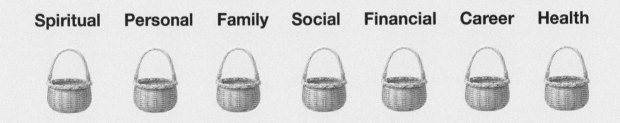

| Spiritual | Personal | Family | Social | Financial | Career | Health |

For this chapter, let's look at the basket of Personal Development. If we want a better life, we have to be better. The Personal Development basket contains many areas. It's broken down into subcategories that we will discuss in two chapters.

MY HOBBIES → SELF CARE → SKILL DEVELOPMENT GOALS

At the end of my life, I will be fulfilled if I regularly make time for these hobbies _____ _____ and learning these skills _____ _____.

The types of self-care most important to me are _____ _____.

In five years, when I look back to this day _____ _____

will have happened for me to be able to say, "Yes! I'm happy and thriving, enjoying life and taking back the pen, writing the rest of my own story."

In one year, I will have _____ _____.

(Examples: gone snow skiing, paddle boarded most weeks, taken more painting lessons, attended a writer's retreat)

In three months, these goals must be done in order to be on track for my one year, five year, and lifetime goals to become a reality:

_____

_____

This week, I will make 3-5 tasks a priority because they are in line with God's will for my life, in line with rest and personal growth. I will rise early and be diligent this week to get these things done in order to make my hobbies, self-care, and learning priorities:

_____

_____

When I get discouraged, I will think of all that I have to be thankful for when it comes to my enjoyment of life. These are a few things I am most thankful for:

_____

_____

DON'T WORRY

BE HAPPY.

"happy™

This is what we will call the H.O.P.E. process. It's the part of Believe ANYWAY where you will dig deeper into the scripture and mine out jewels that I believe God intends to speak to you in profound ways. Find the verses from this chapter that stand out most to you and put these verses through the **H.O.P.E. process.** The "H" stands for **His story.** Simply write out a verse from this chapter. The "O" stands for **Observation.** Ask God to show you what He wants you to observe from this verse the most. Write down what He speaks to you. The "P" stands for **Prayer.** Write out your prayer regarding this verse. What are you needing or wanting to see in your life? Ask Him for it. The "E" is for **Expectation** and this is where you will write out by faith, in present or past tense, what you expect to become reality in your life. Faith is now the substance of things hoped for and the evidence of things not yet seen as Hebrews tells us. This is where our hope turns into faith and brings things from the future into our present.

H IS STORY

_____
_____
_____

O BSERVATION

_____
_____

P RAYER

_____
_____

E XPECTATION

_____
_____

H IS STORY

_____

_____

_____

O BSERVATION

_____

_____

_____

P RAYER

_____

_____

_____

E XPECTATION

_____

_____

_____

H IS STORY

_____

_____

_____

_____

O BSERVATION

_____

_____

_____

P RAYER

_____

_____

_____

E XPECTATION

_____

_____

_____

H IS STORY

_____

_____

_____

O BSERVATION

_____

_____

_____

P RAYER

_____

_____

_____

E XPECTATION

_____

_____

_____

H IS STORY

_____

_____

_____

O BSERVATION

_____

_____

_____

P RAYER

_____

_____

_____

E XPECTATION

_____

_____

_____

Are you a glass half full or a glass half empty person? Note the thought patterns needed to adopt in order to be a Glass Half Full Person. Rate them I-IO according to the priority you plan to focus on to become a Glass Half Full Person

HALF FULL

- God sees ahead and provides
- I am exactly the way God made me for His purpose
- My steps are ordered of the Lord
- I live to give and set my mind on things above
- He will never leave me nor forsake me.

HALF EMPTY

- If only I was more like her
- She has it so good
- I fear my financial future
- What if I end up alone
- I should have...But now regret

I Chose to Believe Anyway...

and this is what happened...

There's a term in the psychology world called "cognitive distortion." Cognitive distortions are defined as twists of the truth within our thoughts. In other words, lies.

Distortions greatly influence our emotions, and they are common in everyday thinking. We all have them. Most of us go around never questioning them simply because we are not aware of them and don't know that we can question them. We end up accepting them as fact and that's where we get into trouble. There is a direct link between cognitive distortions and the prevalence of anxiety, depression, and relationship conflict.

How scary to think that our well-being and the quality of our relationships could be jeopardized by thoughts and beliefs that aren't even true.

So what do you do, once you catch the lie?

Replace it with the truth and allow that to be your guide.

Affirmations are positive statements that help you to challenge and overcome self-sabotaging, negative thoughts. There is science behind this. Studies have shown that affirmations activate the reward centers of the brain, which strengthen the pathways that connect thoughts, emotions, and beliefs. They literally change your mind!

The more you think on something, the deeper it becomes embedded

184

in your mind and will sink down into your heart. Ever catch yourself saying, "I know this is true, but I just don't feel it?" Well, this is how you make that head knowledge become heart knowledge.

And here's the kicker: The key to this, according to research, is that you have to believe it's true. You don't have to feel it, but you absolutely need to believe it.

God's Word is truth. (No wonder the Bible is constantly urging us to meditate on the Word!)

Feelings are fickle and sometimes deceitful, but God's Word never changes and His promises are always true. So, choose to **Believe ANYWAY.**

AMANDA BALENA

Amanda Balena is a Marriage and Family Therapist in Mobile. AL. Through counseling and writing, she strives to help people better enjoy life and relationships. Her website is **www.amandabalena.com**

FAITH WORKS

BY LOVE

WEEK
EIGHT

Believer

I asked my husband what the common, key component was for all of those miracles listed in the chapter on *Crazy Faith*. His answer, without hesitation, was LOVE.

He expounded by saying, "Being so in love with God and His people. And being aware of His love for us all."

His voice cracked as he told me this with such conviction.

SIDENOTE WORTH MENTIONING

He had just been seeking God about miracles flowing out of love. It's so neat when God speaks to us about things around the same time. There is nothing like being married to a faith-filled spouse who loves God more than he loves you. All that faith-filled-love spills out all over you and it's just the best thing ever. I am such a blessed woman. If you are single, wait for your Mr. Wonderful. It takes faith to know it's really love. The two go together very nicely. Faith and love.

Love is the How to Of faith!

You want to live a life that is filled with faith and miracles flowing out of your life? Love is how. "Faith works by love." Galatians 5:6

23"Truly I say to you, whoever says to this mountain, 'Be taken up and cast into the sea,' and does not doubt in his heart, but believes that what he says is going to happen, it will be granted him. 24"Therefore I say to you, all things for which you pray and ask, believe that you have received them, and they will be granted you. 25"Whenever you stand praying, forgive, if you have anything against anyone, so that your Father who is in heaven will also forgive you your transgressions. 26["But if you do not forgive, neither will your Father who is in heaven forgive your transgressions."] Mark 11:23-26 NKJV

Notice that this passage is all about mountain-moving faith.

What short-circuits mountain-moving faith? Choosing not to forgive someone. Another way to say it is by choosing not to *LOVE ANYWAY.*

What keeps us from forgiving? One thing is fear. The Bible tells us that perfect love casts out fear. When we forgive, it sets us free even more so than setting the offender free. Forgiveness doesn't say what was done is okay, or justify it, but it says that you are no longer going to be held hostage by the pain of it any longer. Forgiveness has to be offered by faith. It doesn't always mean you forget. It's okay if there is a sting at the remembrance, but by faith, your heart is clean from it. You simply choose to no longer wish ill will toward anyone or repeat the offense in your head over and over. Taking unforgiving thoughts captive are such a huge part of forgiveness. Casting them over onto Jesus makes our walk lighter and easier. And it strengthens our faith to, literally, then be able to move mountains.

Romans 5:5 tells us that the love of God is shed abroad in our hearts by the Holy Spirit. This means that when we were born again, love came to abide in our hearts, so the love of God is in us. We have to choose to yield to it instead of jealousy, or being offended, or strife, or unforgiveness.

The very last chapter of Love ANYWAY explains this in great detail. All of the fruits of the Spirit flow out of love. The fruits work together to help us be who we are called to be, as Christians. And the fruit of patience is especially helpful when yielded to by faith. It has been said that faith and patience are the power twins.

> When we are standing in faith for something and need the power of God to show up in our lives to create change in some way, often we also need to yield to patience. Have you ever noticed? God is not always on our timetable. Can I get an AMEN?

Another fruit that helps to undergird our faith is peace. The Bible tells us that the peace of God passes understanding, meaning it makes zero-sense to have that much peace at certain times. I remember during an uncertain season that a friend of mine was flabbergasted by my peace level. The thing is, if it becomes second nature to you to yield to peace, when all hell is breaking lose, you don't even notice. Even when those around you, who are grasping for it, take note. When you are genuinely convinced God has your back, it is far more easy to lean into peace. I wish I could say friends would always think this of me. Not the case. I am normal and don't always yield to peace, but this time was so clear to me and has been a great reference for when I was not in peace. I think back to this story, and by choice, move out of anxiety, stress, and worry back into peace.

We can also learn how to follow peace by faith when we are needing to know where God is leading us. Maybe, for example, if you are trying to decide on a career path or a job change or some big directional decision. The best way to know which way to go at a crossroads in life is to follow peace. What do I mean by this? When you pray and ask God if you should go this direction, and you sense more peace than when you pray about going the other direction.

Our hearts know which way to go if we are in living in regular contact with God.

His sheep know His voice and the voice of a stranger will not harken. So whichever direction brings peace, go that way. I was in an interview recently with someone, and by the end of it, there was such a lack of peace I was almost nauseated. I felt like I might pass out. Yet in another interview, there was peace, and I chose to hire the person. The other person seemed more qualified. At first, I was so unsure of which way to go, but I am so glad I went with peace because the person I hired has hustled and is hungry to learn and grow.

Some of the top hindrances of faith are pride, fear, and unforgiveness. Pride is the hindrance of these three we haven't discussed yet, so let's hit pride right between the eyes...or should I say "ii's?

Pride comes in lots of forms such as false humility, being judgmental, leaning on our own understanding, not acknowledging God in all our ways, not enough-ness and shame to name a few. The angle I want us to look at is simple self-awareness and what true humility looks like. The married couples having serious issues, which we are not sure if we can help or not, are the ones who know more than us when we try to share wisdom with them, who have no self-awareness, and who talk more than they listen. Simply put, they won't get under what they need to get under so they can get over what they need to get over. It seriously astonishes me when people pay money to go and sit and hear a therapist tell them what the problem is, and then they come to us (for free) and tell us how that therapist isn't helping them and how they just don't understand their "oh so special" situation.

I want to scream: NEWS FLASH! LISTEN TO ME. I am not the one here with the marriage falling apart and neither is your therapist. You are!! You are full of pride and think you know it all. I don't say that out loud - ever. I just think about it sometimes.

These are also the same people who will say, "I just don't think our situation can be healed." The worst of marriages can be healed. But the very first step is to BELIEVE they can be. This is point I am trying to drive home! You will only be able to believe to the degree that you choose to love and let your faith be expressed for each other through that love. Then, and only then, can your marriage thrive like you so desperately want it to. I know this is easier to read the words, than to live them out! But I have done both. I'm telling you, there is hope. Unfortunately, I've accurately described dozens of couples who have visited our office over the last twenty-five years. This is common, and yet so fixable with an open heart able to crucify fear, pride, and unforgiveness. You are capable of believing anyway in your marriage again.

We all have the same measure of faith, so you already have enough. Don't believe the lie that you don't. We all deal with the same general problems. Yours are no more special than mine and vice versa. Life is just super hard for us all at times. Total surrender to love by faith is how to overcome. We were not promised the absence of the presence of problems, but we were promised the power to overcome by love!

Love is action packed. Love is a verb. Cliché or not, it's true. How is this the case? Because love does. Love Believes ANYWAY in people who don't deserve it and in dreams that are way out there or seemingly dead. James 2 talks about faith without the works of love being dead. You want your faith to never fail? Put your faith in love and let it be your works of love, because love never fails!

Faith that works by love causes us to thrive in life. It's the only way we please God. God knows that faith is the currency that works in a system of Love. This currency is what we use to believe for everything we need.

Here's some exciting news that will boost your faith and help you to believe ANYWAY and thrive in life:

We win!
I read the back of the book!

"But what matters is a faith that expresses itself through love"

Galatians 5:6(GWT)

Believe

The Science of Believing:

As I was writing Happy ANYWAY, I stumbled upon a most amazing study, called the Harvard Grant Study. You may have heard me talk about this if you have attended any Happy Girl Conferences or read Happy ANYWAY, Love ANYWAY, or are subscribed to my Happy Monday Blog. But just in case you are new to the happy sisterhood, this is going to rock your world. This study is said to be one of the most comprehensive studies in history. The seventy-five-year-long study scientifically reveals the secret to a happy and fulfilled life and verifies just how important this topic is.

Dr. George Vaillant, who led the study for thirty-eight of the years, concluded that there are two pillars of happiness, "One is love. The other is finding a way of coping with life that does not push love away." He goes on to say the study points to a straightforward conclusion: "Happiness is love. Full stop." So, there you have it. A person may have all the luxuries the world has to offer; but without love, they don't mean a whole lot. This study that began in 1938 spanning seventy-five years, expended twenty million dollars to find out that love is the key to a happy life.

I love how science simply further proves out scripture.

1 John 4:8 tells us God is love and 1 Corinthians 13:8 says Love never fails. Of course, they found that Love is the secret to a happy life, because God is love and love never fails. God is the secret to a happy life! It all makes perfect sense, doesn't it?

Don't Stop Believing!

Spiritual	Personal	Family	Social	Financial	Career	Health

For this chapter, let's finally take a look at the Spiritual basket of your life. We saved the most important basket for last. If this basket isn't intact, you can hang it up. Nothing else will really work until this area of life is healthy. So, let's go deeper into the things of God together. Let's get real and as you go through this exercise, shake off any shame or regrets. Only let yourself look toward the future - starting with right now. I pray your walk with God is richer than it has ever been as a result of this exercise.

MY SPIRITUAL GOALS

At the end of my life, I will measure the effectiveness and fulfillment of my walk with God by this:

_____.

In five years, when I look back to this day _____

_____

will have happened for me to be able to say, "Yes! I have a solid, healthy walk with God."

In one year, I will be able to describe my walk with God like this: _____

_____ .

In three months, these goals must be accomplished in order to be on track for my one year, five year, and lifetime spiritual goals to become a reality: _____

_____

This week I will make 3-5 tasks a priority because they will help me grow spiritually and bear more fruit in my Christian walk. I will rise early and be diligent this week to get these things done in order to reach my goals:

_____

_____

(Examples: pray, journal, read the Bible daily, gratitude list, serve at church weekly, join a small group)

When I get discouraged, I will think of all that I have to be thankful for when it comes to my walk with God. These are few things I am most thankful for:

_____

_____

ONE STEP OUT OF

Love

IS ONE STEP OUT OF

God.

KENNETH E. HAGIN

This is what we will call the H.O.P.E. process. It's the part of Believe ANYWAY where you will dig deeper into the scripture and mine out jewels that I believe God intends to speak to you in profound ways. Find the verses from this chapter that stand out most to you and put these verses through the **H.O.P.E. process.** The "H" stands for **His story.** Simply write out a verse from this chapter. The "O" stands for **Observation**. Ask God to show you what He wants you to observe from this verse the most. Write down what He speaks to you. The "P" stands for **Prayer.** Write out your prayer regarding this verse. What are you needing or wanting to see in your life? Ask Him for it. The "E" is for **Expectation** and this is where you will write out by faith, in present or past tense, what you expect to become reality in your life. Faith is now the substance of things hoped for and the evidence of things not yet seen as Hebrews tells us. This is where our hope turns into faith and brings things from the future into our present.

H IS STORY

_____
_____

O BSERVATION

_____
_____

P RAYER

_____
_____

E XPECTATION

_____
_____

H IS STORY

_____
_____
_____

O BSERVATION

_____
_____
_____

P RAYER

_____
_____
_____

E XPECTATION

_____
_____
_____

H IS STORY

_____
_____
_____
_____

O BSERVATION

_____
_____
_____
_____

P RAYER

_____
_____
_____
_____

E XPECTATION

_____
_____
_____
_____

H IS STORY

_____

_____

_____

O BSERVATION

_____

_____

_____

P RAYER

_____

_____

_____

E XPECTATION

_____

_____

_____

H IS STORY

_____

_____

_____

O BSERVATION

_____

_____

_____

P RAYER

_____

_____

_____

E XPECTATION

_____

_____

_____

In what ways can you see that Love will help you overcome your biggest obstacle in life right now? Example: spending more time with _____ instead of watching tv. In what ways can you fill your love tank to have all the fuel needed to believe ANYWAY in God and in yourself to see your dreams come true? Use the blank canvas to draw a picture of something that fills your love tank.

I Chose to Believe Anyway...

and this is what happened...

She was fifteen years old, attending youth church camp in Eupora, Mississippi. She was beautiful, athletic, and brunette. She was my "type." As we sat around the Olympic-sized swimming pool during the water-baptism service, she was wishing she could be baptized along with dozens of teens that day.

But there was a problem: She was wearing a white tee shirt. So instead she simply prayed and dedicated her heart to the Lord.

In the same exact moment, across the pool, this eighties, mullet-headed boy jumped up and announced, "The Lord just spoke to me that there's a girl who wants to be baptized, but she can't because she's in a white tee shirt. If that's you, take my purple t-shirt!" She stood up with tears flowing down her cheeks shouting, "It's me! I want to be baptized." So that summer day in 1986, she was baptized. That boy was me, and that gorgeous brunette is now my wife, Adrienne Massey Cooley, and the author of this incredible book. And no, I never got the shirt back, but it was worth it.

A year passed by. I preached in her youth group across town. That night I spoke on purity and the Lord spoke to her to stop dating. (Thanks, God! I was going to ask her out.) So another year went by and I spoke in her youth group. Afterwards, about twenty of us went for pizza. She and I started hanging out and that summer we were inseparable. I knew then I would marry this girl some day.

Fast forward...I graduated high school,

went to Bible School and she graduated and went to college. For two years, she lived "the college life" and I prayed for her. I would call and leave voicemails in her college dorm room. She would come in from partying, hear the messages, and be convicted because she knew she had a call of God on her life for ministry.

I finished Bible College and moved to India as a missionary. I decided to settle there permanently so my "Indian Parents" agreed to arrange a marriage with a lovely Indian girl. But before we were engaged, I began to have dreams about Adrienne for three nights in a row. So I decided to write her a letter reminding her of the call on her life. Months later she read the letter and the next Sunday went to church, cried through the announcements, and rededicated her life to Christ.

I felt led to go back home and reached out to her one last time.

When I did, she told me she had gotten my letter and was so thankful for my prayers. She dropped out of nursing school with an almost full scholarship and went to Bible School to pursue Ministry. Fifteen months later we were married.

There are so many more fun details to our story, but to sum it up, she is the woman of my dreams! Literally! Even in situations that look impossible, the key is to go on with God, trust Him, and just like He brought us back together and has given us a happily-ever-after, **Believe ANYWAY** and He will do the same for you. He will turn your impossibilities into reality!

He will cause you to thrive no matter what life throws at you!

KEVIN COOLEY

Lead Pastor
Harvest Church, Mobile, AL
Founder & President
Embassy of Hope &
Kevin Cooley Ministries, Inc.

Believe ANYWAY Summarized

(Tear these pages out after you read the book and put it on your mirror to remind you to live the life of your dreams believing ANYWAY!)

SEE IT & BE IT

"For as {s}he thinks in her heart so is {s}he..."
Proverbs 23:7 NKJ

✓ make a vision board
✓ get a daily success routine
✓ imagine living your best life
✓ write and review your goals daily
✓ **believe ANYWAY**

OUR SECRET WEAPON

"The effective, fervent prayer of a righteous {wo}man avails much." James 5:16b NKJV

✓ declare His Word
✓ understand the power behind the name of Jesus
✓ pray without ceasing
✓ fully expect to receive
✓ **believe ANYWAY**

WHEN ALL HOPE IS LOST

"Under utterly hopeless circumstances {s}he hopefully believed..." Romans 4:18, WNT

✓ deal with your emotions, don't ignore them
✓ get help if needed
✓ focus on what you have and can do
✓ remind yourself pain won't kill you
✓ **believe ANYWAY**

CRAZY FAITH

"He who is in you is greater than he who is in the world."
1 John 4:4b NKJV

✓ remind yourself of God's faithfulness
✓ fill yourself with His Word
✓ don't back down to impossibilities
✓ jump out into the deep
✓ **believe ANYWAY**

OBEY NOW. UNDERSTAND LATER.

**"Trust in the Lord with all your heart and lean not on your own understanding."
Proverbs 3:5 NIV**

- ✓ stop trying to figure it all out
- ✓ be teachable
- ✓ humble yourself
- ✓ don't be moved by what you see
- ✓ **believe ANYWAY**

HAPPY PEOPLE TRUST THE LORD

"Happy are those who trust in the Lord." Psalm 40:4 GNB

- ✓ don't worry, be happy
- ✓ choose a happy perspective
- ✓ develop happy habits
- ✓ improve your health by being happy
- ✓ **believe ANYWAY**

I STILL BELIEVE

**"And we know that all things work together for good to those who love God, to those who are the called according to His purpose."
Romans 8:28 NKJV**

- ✓ trust Him in the storm
- ✓ stay rooted and grounded no matter what
- ✓ sing of His promises
- ✓ be thankful
- ✓ **believe ANYWAY**

FAITH WORKS BY LOVE

"But what matters is a faith that expresses itself through love." Galatians 5:6 GWT

- ✓ love God with all your heart
- ✓ receive His love
- ✓ love you well, so you can love them well
- ✓ yield to love & overcome anything
- ✓ **believe ANYWAY**

I pray you walk in a new level of faith and never lose hope by choosing to **believe ANYWAY** no matter what life throws at you!

I hope you have enjoyed **Believe Anyway** as much as I enjoyed writing it! I put my whole heart into it.

WANT MORE?

You can also get Happy Anyway or Love Anyway on Amazon or at my website at **adriennecooley.com**

HAPPY GIRL CONFERENCE is a conference I host and am so thankful to have amazing speakers each year like Lisa Young, Terri Savelle Foy, Pattie Duininc, Peppi Sims and others. God always sends just the right message to spread the happy, share the love and spark purpose in the lives of those who join the fun!

I hope you will join us this upcoming year. You can find out the details at adriennecooley.com and subscribe to my *#HappyMondayBlog* there, too!

See you in your inbox!

Follow me on social media so we can stay connected!

Facebook: Adrienne Cooley
Instagram & Twitter: @addiecooley

CPSIA information can be obtained
at www.ICGtesting.com
Printed in the USA
BVHW061012070921
616216BV00018B/455

9 781937 250676